Great Priest Imhotep

MAKOTO MORISHITA

Great Priest Imhotep

"NETJERIKHET"?
IT MEANS "DIVINE BODY."
IT IS YOUR TRUE NAME.
FUEEEH!!? SERIOUSLY!? THAT'S WHAT IT IS!!?
THAT'S WAY COOL!!!
DO NOT TELL A SOUL.
TRUE NAME: A SECRET NAME KNOWN ONLY BY ONE'S MOTHER. IF SOMEONE KNOWS YOUR TRUE NAME, YOU ARE EASIER TO CURSE OR OTHERWISE AFFECT WITH MAGIC.
WAIT, HOW COME YOU KNOW MY TRUE NAME??
BECAUSE I AM A GREAT PRIEST.
OH YEAH?
IN TRUTH, IT WAS TOLD TO ME SO THAT YOU, OUR HUMAN SACRIFICE, CANNOT ESCAPE.
?
......IT IS A SNIDE NAME.
ALMOST ...
...AS IF TO TELL YOU, "YOUR BODY BELONGS TO THE GODS."

SCROLL 40: WE'RE NOT FRIENDS ANYMORE!!!

Great Priest Imhotep

I DON'T REALLY MIND, THOUGH.
BEIN' A "DIVINE BODY."
WHAT ???
THERE ARE OTHERS IN THIS WORLD WHO OFFER UP THE ENTIRETY OF THEIR LIVES AS THE GODS' VESSELS.
COULD YOU STILL SAY THAT IF THE SAME HAPPENED TO YOU!?
ERK !!!
...COME AGAIN?
WELL, YEAH, I DON'T WANNA GIVE OVER MY ENTIRE LIFE...
...BUT EVEN THE GODS MUST WANNA CHAT FACE-TO-FACE WITH THEIR FRIENDS, RIGHT?
GODS... HAVING FRIENDS?
SO, LIKE...
...IF IT MEANT I COULD HELP 'EM OUT WITH THAT...
...I'D GLADLY LEND 'EM MY BODY!!
YOU ARE...
DJOSER.

...TOO KIND.

KH KH KH!

AH HA HA HA HA HA HA HA!

CLINK

FORGET BEING HIS VIZIER...

...YOU WEREN'T EVEN WORTHY TO BE HIS BEST FRIEND, WERE YAAA!!!?

I WILL MAKE HIS DREAMS REALITY ...!!

EVER SINCE THE DAY I VOWED SO AND CROSSED ARMS WITH HIM...

...IT HAS BEEN MY ROLE TO SUPPORT HIM AS THE MOON SUPPORTS THE SUN ...!!

APOPHIS !!!!

YOU HAVE NO RIGHT TO SQUAT IN MY PHARAOH'S BODY!
LEAVE IT AT ONCE !!!
I WILL FINALLY SAVE YOU ...!!!
WHUMP
BOLD WORDS FROM A MAN WITHOUT A PLAN.
LEMME FILL YOU IN ON THE SURFACE WORLD SITUATION RIGHT NOW.
ZUM ZUM ZUM ZUM ZUM ZUM ZUM ZUM ZUM
WAAAAAAAAH!

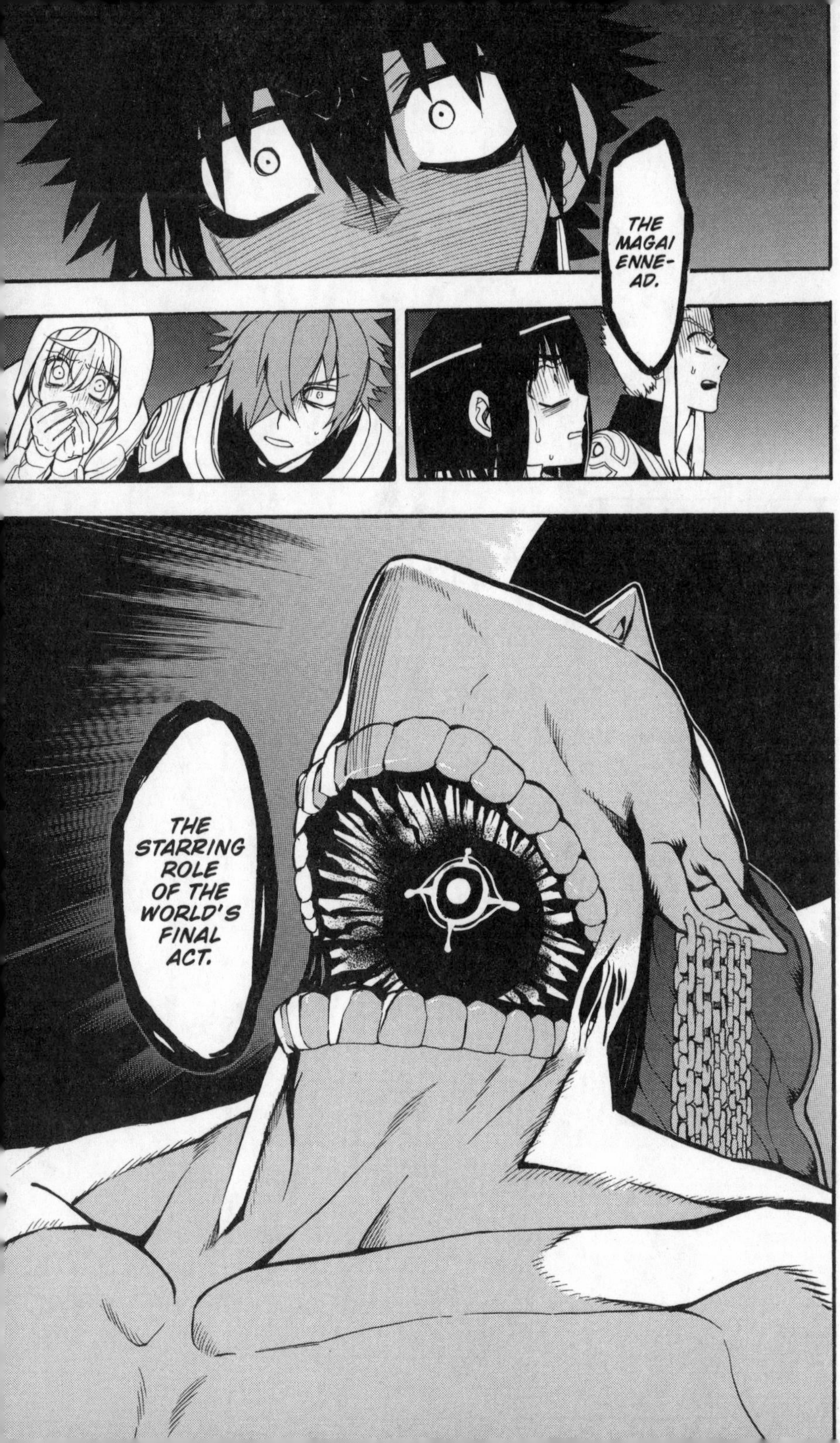

THE STARRING ROLE OF THE WORLD'S FINAL ACT.

KATHOOM
AH-HA-HA-HA-HA-HA-HA-HA-HA-HA-HA-HA-HA-HA!
NOOOOOO!
HELP!
UGH!
URRK!
OOF!
AHH... AHHH!!! IT'S ALL COMIN' BACK!!!
RUUUUMBLE
DROP

SO MANY DEATHS-SSS!!!
THE PIECES OF ME ARE COMING BACK...
...FROM THE DEAD HUMANS' SOULS! OH, I CAN FEEEEEL IT!!!
AH-HA-HA-HA-HA-HA-HA-HA!
SHUDDER
YOU SON OF A ...!!!
IMHO-TEP!!!
WE HAVE TO TAKE DOWN THIS EVIL GOD NOW!
WAIT! THERE'S NO TELLING WHAT POWER HE'S GAINED!!
DO NOT BE RASH—
OH!!?

I CAN NAME OFF EXACTLY WHO'S DIED TOO!!!
NASIRE SULE-MAN.
FAHAD SALEH.
FARUQ RAMZI.
TAOUFIK GEB.
ADRIA MILLER.
CHEN LI.
ZOE LETHAM.
TEÓDORO NAZARIO.
HISATOYO SAIZONO.
ELSA EHREN.
KATSUYA SAIGA.
AN MITSU-KIDE.

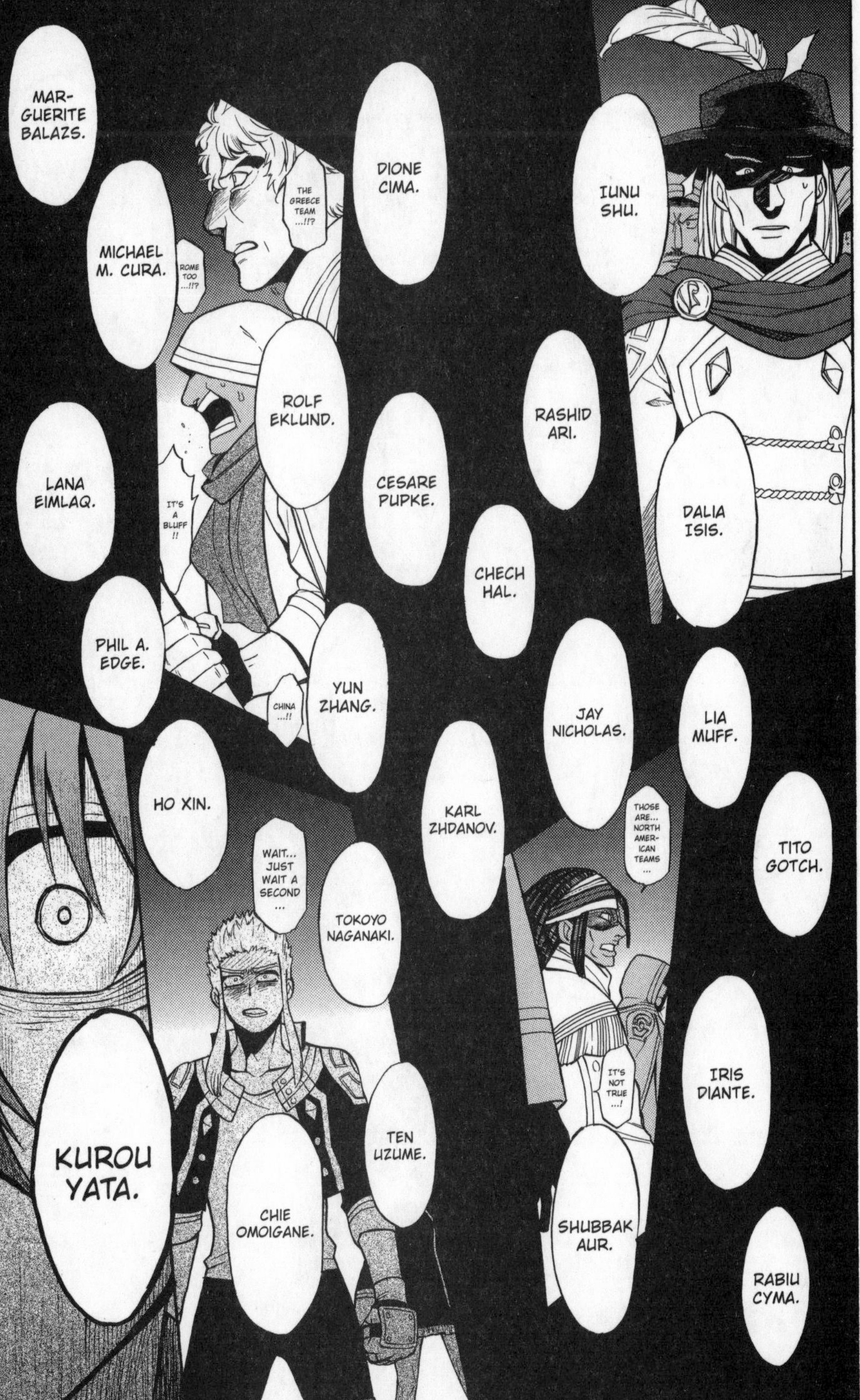
IUNU SHU.
DIONE CIMA.
THE GREECE TEAM ...!!?
MARGUERITE BALAZS.
MICHAEL M. CURA.
ROME TOO ...!!?
RASHID ARI.
DALIA ISIS.
CESARE PUPKE.
ROLF EKLUND.
IT'S A BLUFF !!
LANA EIMLAQ.
CHECH HAL.
YUN ZHANG.
CHINA ...!!
PHIL A. EDGE.
TITO GOTCH.
LIA MUFF.
JAY NICHOLAS.
THOSE ARE... NORTH AMERICAN TEAMS ...
KARL ZHDANOV.
TOKOYO NAGANAKI.
WAIT... JUST WAIT A SECOND ...
HO XIN.
RABIU CYMA.
IRIS DIANTE.
IT'S NOT TRUE ...!
SHUBBAK AUR.
TEN UZUME.
CHIE OMOIGANE.
KUROU YATA.

RYUU KUGA-SHIRA.
KOBUSHI SHIRAHANA.
HUH? THE PRIEST-HOOD HQ STILL HASN'T FALLEN?
THE STRAGGLERS ARE HAULING BUTT TO PROTECT THE ENNEAD, I BET.
BUT...

...RIGHT ABOUT NOW, JUST HOLDING THE WORLD TOGETHER IS PROBABLY THE BEST THEY CAN DO.
KRAK

OHHH MAN... THE COFFIN-MAKERS ARE GONNA MAKE A KILLING TOMORROW! ♪

IF TOMORROW EVER COMES, THAT IS.

HEY, LADIES AND GENTS!!
IT'S THE FINAL ACT AND YOU'RE JUST STANDING THERE WATCHING A LIVE BROADCAST! ISN'T THAT A WASTE!?

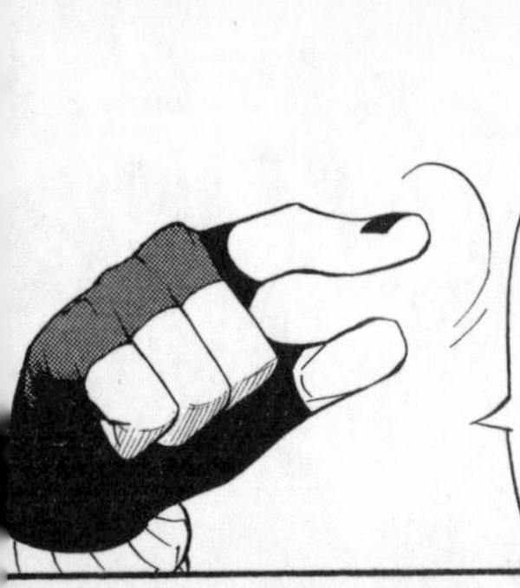

THEN IT FOL-LOWS...

...THAT YOU'D MAKE HELLA STRONG MAGAI TOO!!!

SNAP

!!?

THUD

WHAM

ZUM
ZUM
ARGH...!!?
ZUM
ZUM
GAAH!
ZUM
ZUM
ZUZUM
AHHH!
AH!
NO!
I DON'T EVEN NEED TO USE THOSE PAIN-IN-THE-BUTT PILLS ANYMORE.

THOTH !!!
LET ME USE DAMNATIO MEMORI-AE!!
I BEG OF YOU !!!
......
THOTH!!? ANSWER ME!!!
WHY !!?
ENOUGH WITH THE WAILING.
C'MON, THOTH. YOU'VE SEEN THE LIGHT NOW, RIGHT?
AAAAAAAAAAAAAAAA
YOU SEE THESE MORTALS DON'T STAND A CHANCE, RIIIIIGHT ???
THOTH !!!
...DO YOU THINK YOU CAN CAST THAT SPELL FOR FREE?
CALM DOWN.

A MAGIC SPELL TO REWRITE THE WORLD'S RECORDS...

IT WAS ONLY MEANT TO BE USED ONCE.

WE'VE USED IT TWICE NOW, EVEN IF ONLY ON A SMALL SCALE.

ANY MORE UNNATURAL REWRITING COULD BRING ABOUT A GLITCH IN THE WORLD ITSELF!

WE WOULD ONLY BE HELPING APOPHIS!

...BE-SIDES, IT'S NO USE.

EVEN IF WE ERASED THIS EVENT, THEY'D BE TURNED INTO MAGAI AGAIN AND AGAIN.

YOU CAN FORCE THEM TO REPEATEDLY ENDURE THE SUFFERING OF THEIR TRANSFORMA-TION INTO MAGAI...

..OR GIVE THEM PEACE. WHICH WOULD YOU PREFER!?

YOU MUST BE JOK-ING!!!

THEY ARE ALL MY COMRADES!!! DJOSER IS NOT THE ONLY ONE I WISH TO PROTECT!!!

BOOM

THE HELL... ARE YOU WAITIN' AROUND FOR...!?
I TOLD YOU I'D KILL 'IM DEAD, REMEM-BER...!?

!!?

DIDN'T I EXPLAIN THIS ALREADY?
SWISH

DON'T UNDER-ESTIMATE HUMAN VENGEFUL-NESS...!!!

I AM THE PHARAOH OF THE MAGAI.

STOP...
...FIGHTING! PLEASE!!!

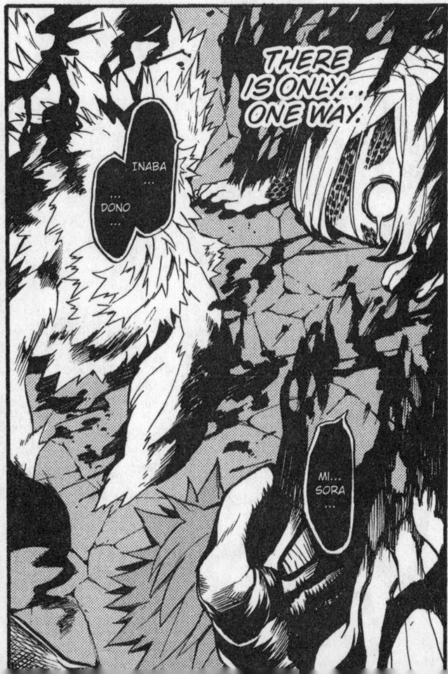

NII-SA...
SPLURT

IS THAT EVERY-BODY?
STOP IIIIIT!
DAMMIIIIIIT!
GIVE UP ON THEM.

FLASH
CLATTER

HEY, THANKS! ♪
THANKS TO YOU BRINGIN' SO MANY PEOPLE HERE...
...I GOT TO GIVE IMHOTEP THE ULTIMATE ANTI-GIFT!

HUH?
THERE'S SOME-BODY WHO HASN'T TURNED?
OHH, I SEE!
RIGHT! YOUR KA WAS A MAGAI FROM THE GET-GO!!

EVERYBODY... TURNED INTO MAGAI...!

GH !!?
WAAAH!
SHWOOP
SHWOOP

TMP
OH, *THOOOTH*? ARE YOU STILL NOT GONNA WAKE THE OGDOAD, AFTER SEEIN' ALL THISSS?

......

HOW IS KILLIN' THE OGDOAD GONNA HARM YOU ANYWAY? IT'S NOT LIKE YOU'D DIE.
IT'S TIME TO LEAVE THE NEST, BUDDY!

DE-STRUCTION AS AN END UNTO ITSELF...
IS THAT NOT UTTERLY POINT-LESS?

...AFTER YOU'VE DESTROYED THIS WORLD... WHAT IS IT YOU WISH TO DO...?

...Y'KNOW, MAN... IT'S THE OBLIVIOUS VILLAINS WHO SPOUT OFF RIGHTEOUS-SOUNDING LINES LIKE THAT.

THE TRUTH IS, YOU DESPISE ME, DON'T YOU!?

I AM YOUR FRIEND... YET I ALWAYS OBEYED MY INSTRUCTIONS, NOT MY HEART. I NEVER SAVED YOU!

I KNEW THE SECRET BEHIND YOUR IMMORTALITY, YET I NEVER SAID A WORD TO YOU!

DON'T YOU WANT TO KILL ME TOO!!?

WITHOUT THE OGDOAD, I'LL HAVE NO REASON TO EXIST.

IF YOU ARE GOING TO ERASE THEM, THEN ERASE ME TOO.

I'M NOT GONNA ERASE YOU, BUD.

WE'RE FRIENDS!

THAT MAKES YOU SPECIAL.

I WANNA FORGIVE YOU 'SPECIALLY.

AND I 'SPECIALLY CAN'T FORGIVE YOU.

TUG
THAT'S WHY I DECIDED ...
...TO HAVE YOU LIVE ON FOREVER, THOTH.
I'LL MAKE YOU WATCH ME WIN.
I'LL MAKE YOU WATCH UNTIL THE LAST MOMENT, WHEN I END MY OWN LIFE.
YOU'LL BE ALL ALONE IN THE WORLD AT THE VERY END.
THAT'S YOUR PUNISH-MENT FOR ABANDON-ING ME!!

"OBLIVIOUS...
...VILLAIN."

THE ONE WHO MOST BROKE YOU...
WHO MOST DROVE YOU TO MADNESS...
WAS IT...?
HAAAH... HAAAH...
!!?
ROAR

AH!
STOP!! HINOME!!
RYUU...
KOBUSHI......
SCRAPE
ALL OF THEM!
GIVE THEM BACK!!
ROOOAR

SEKH-MET'S FLAMES, EH?

SHOOM

"BLACK FIRE"!!!

HINOMEEE!!!
ONEE-CHA-AAN!

SURELY YOU AREN'T THROWING FLAMES AT A FORMER SUN GOD, NOW ARE YOUUUU!!?

THAT'S WEIRD.
SHE SUR-VIVED THE FI...
THROB
!!?

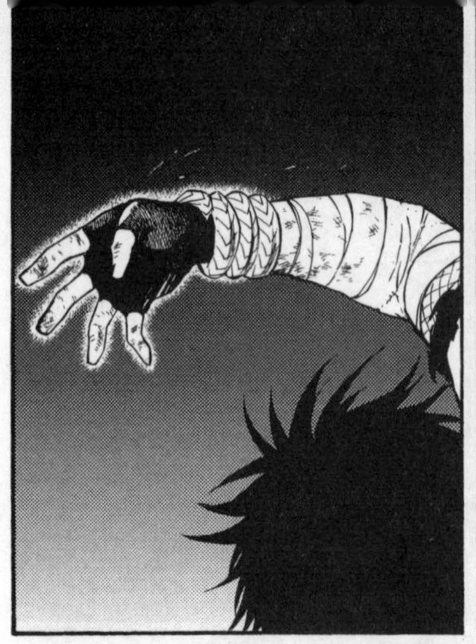

...HEY, KHONSU-KUN.
CAN I ASK YA TO CLEAN UP FOR ME?

THAT HUMAN...
...IS THE BIGGEST WRENCH IN OUR PLAN.

...YOU SCARED?

HUH?

"ASETOS"— HEALING LIGATURE OF THE GODDESS!!!
SHIIINE
UNTIL NOW...
...I NEVER HAD A REASON TO FIGHT. NOT ONE I'D CHOSEN FOR MYSELF.
THOTH ...?
"I AM MERELY A GUARDIAN OF THE OGDOAD."
"I AM AN OBSERVER."
I WAS MAKING EXCUSES. FLEEING TO A POSITION FROM WHICH I NEED NOT TAKE ANY SIDE.
BUT...
...I'VE FINALLY CHOSEN.

I WILL FIGHT...

...TO NEVER LET YOU BE ALONE AGAIN!!!

NOT LEAVING YOU ALONE...
...MEANS I WILL NOT BE ALONE EITHER!!
I CANNOT OBEY YOUR REQUEST...
...APOPHIS!

...!
RISE
DO NOT DESPAIR.

EVEN IF WE LOSE HUMAN FORM...
...WE ARE COMRADES.
...?

IMHO-TEP.
I WILL FIGHT APOPHIS.
!!

YOU...
...SAVE DJOSER.

...UNDER-STOOD!

AH...
AH HA! HA HA HA!
HA HA...!!
NOW...
TREMBLE
TREMBLE
...AFTER I BE-TRAYED YOU...
...OF ALL TIMES ......!!?
RATTLE
THOSE WORDS... ...I WANTED TO HEAR BACK THEN...
YOU'RE GONNA SAY 'EM NOW...?
FRIENDS MAKE UP...
...AFTER A FIGHT, DO THEY NOT?
I REEE-ALLY...
...REALLY...
...CAN'T FORGIVE YOU...!!!

WE'RE NOT FRIENDS ANY-MORE !!!

Great Priest Imhotep

Great Priest Imhotep

SCROLL 41: RETURN OF THE KING
Imhotep.

Great Priest Imhotep

...A NEW TERM FOR US?

AREN'T WE ALREADY THE OGDOAD'S "GUARDIAN GODS"?

THAT IS A TERM THAT DENOTES OUR RELATIONSHIP TO OUR MASTERS.

AS THOTH, THE INDIVIDUAL...

...I WANTED TO CREATE A NEW "WORD" FOR MY RELATIONSHIP WITH YOU!

A "WORD" TO CONNECT YOU AND I.

LISTEN, APOPHIS.

LET'S BE "FRIENDS"!

HOW DO YOU PLAN TO DEFEAT HIM, THOTH!?
OUR TARGET IS HIS CHEST.

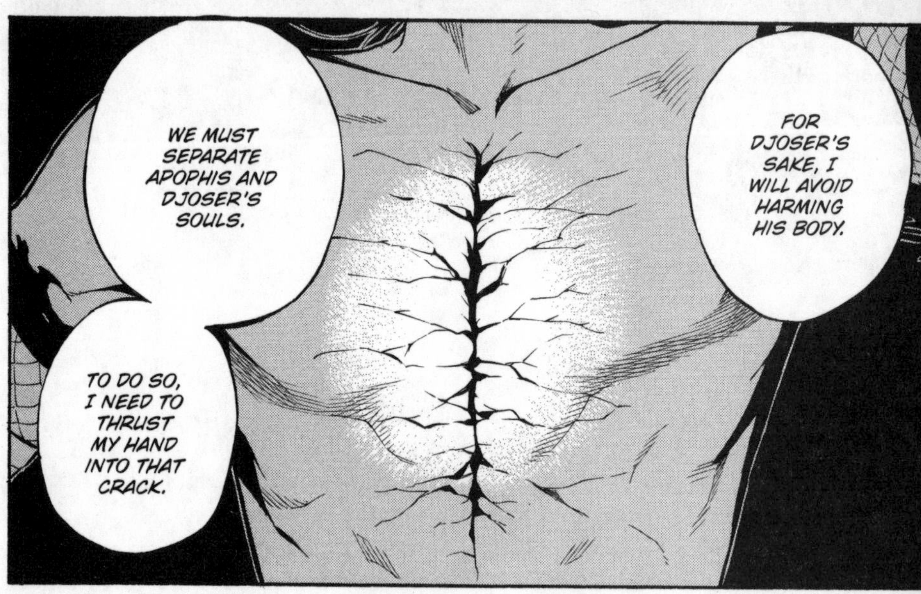
FOR DJOSER'S SAKE, I WILL AVOID HARMING HIS BODY.
WE MUST SEPARATE APOPHIS AND DJOSER'S SOULS.
TO DO SO, I NEED TO THRUST MY HAND INTO THAT CRACK.

I'LL TOUCH THE SOUL DIRECTLY, AND REWRITE IT SO THAT THE MERGING OF THEIR TWO SOULS NEVER HAPPENED!
WITH DAMNATIO MEMORIAE!? BUT THAT COULD...!
IF I TOUCH IT DIRECTLY, I CAN LIMIT THE SPELL'S EFFECTS AND PREVENT IT FROM CAUSING A GLITCH IN THE WORLD.
ONCE THEY'RE SEPARATED, ALL THAT'S LEFT IS TO DRIVE APOPHIS OUT OF THE BODY.
SHOULD WE SUCCEED, APOPHIS WILL LOSE THE BODY—HIS ARMOR—AND HALF OF HIS SOUL!

"BLACK HOLE" !!!
WHRRL
KUH ...!!!
!!
AHH!!
IMMMM!!!
YOU ARE TOO OBVI-OUS...
...THOOOTH!!!!
...IS WHAT YOU'RE THINKIN', RIGHT?
!!!

YOU ARE TOO OBVIOUS...
CLICK
...THOOOOTH!!!!

!!?
EH!?
WHAT!?
BUT... HE WAS JUST SUCKED INTO THE...!
GLARE
SEE!!?
YOU CAME BAAACK!!!

"MOON-WALK."
YOUR SIGNATURE MOVE—SLIPPING THROUGH SPACE-TIME...
...BY OH-SO-CASUALLY REWRITING THE PAST AND FUTURE!!

I CAN READ YOU...
...LIKE AN OPEN BOOK!!
SHWOO

NOW, UNTIL MY PLAY IS OVER...
...STAY IN THE AUDIENCE!!
BLAZE
!!!?
EH...!!?
TCH...!!
YOU LIT-TLE...!
SWING
SWING

DO YOU REALLY HAVE TIME TO BE THINKING!!? DO YOU, THOOOTH!!?

WAIT...

HE ACTED ODD THEN TOO.

!!?

"SEKHMET'S FLAMES." A SUN GODDESS.

MAGICAL POWER WITH A SUN ATTRIBUTE...

COULD IT BE—

DJOSER...
BURST
ARE YOU FIGHTING?
!!!
CLICK
HINOME!!
ME!?
FIRE SEKHMET'S FLAMES AT HIM!!!
IN A FRENZY IS FINE!
JUST HIT HIM WITH IT!!
IM!?
HAAAH!?

THE SUN-SOUL AND THE SUN'S FLAMES BOTH POSSESS THE SAME MAGIC ENERGY!!

IF DJOSER TOOK HINOME'S MAGIC, AND IS FIGHTING BACK INSIDE, THEN...!!

APOPHIS CANNOT ABSORB HER FLAMES ANYMORE!!

I'LL STRIKE !!!
NOW !!!
WHOOSH
"SEKHMETEOR" !!!
ROOOAR
HE'S DIS-TRACTED !!!
THIS IS MY CHANCE ...!!

TOO HASTY.

WHAM

DON'T FORCE THE SAC-RIFICES ONTO OTHERS ...
...WHILE MAKING NO SAC-RIFICES OF YOUR OWN!!

CRUMBLE
CRUMBLE

CRUMBLE
CRUMBLE

WHOOPS!

MY BAAAD!
DIDJA GET CAUGHT UP IN THAT?

HFF...
I CAN'T USE MOONWALK ANYMORE.
I CAN ONLY AFFORD TO REWRITE EVENTS ONE MORE TIME...
...AND I MUST USE THAT ONE TIME TO SEPARATE DJOSER FROM APOPHIS'S SOUL...!
HFF...

THUMP
GAAAAH!
WHOOM
I...
...WAS SHOCKED, Y'KNOW?
YOU'D NEVER HAD ANY FRIENDS OTHER THAN ME...
...YET YOU PULLED TOGETHER THAT AWFULLY RAGTAG BUNCH OF ALLIES.
GOOD JOB, THOTH.
......!!
WAS YOUR LITTLE REBELLIOUS PHASE FUN?
JUST WHEN I WAS PUMPED TO SEE YOU FINALLY DISOBEY OUR PARENT GODS' INSTRUCTIONS...
HSSS
...TO TOP IT ALL OFF...
...YOU CHOSE TO SIDE WITH THE "HUMANS"?

I MEAN, THEY'RE HUMANS ...!!
THE CREATURES WHO FIRST CALLED ME AN "EVIL GOD"...!!!
WHY... DID YOU SIDE WITH THOSE NASTY HUMANS ...!!?
INSTEAD OF ME, YOUR "FRIEND" ...!!?

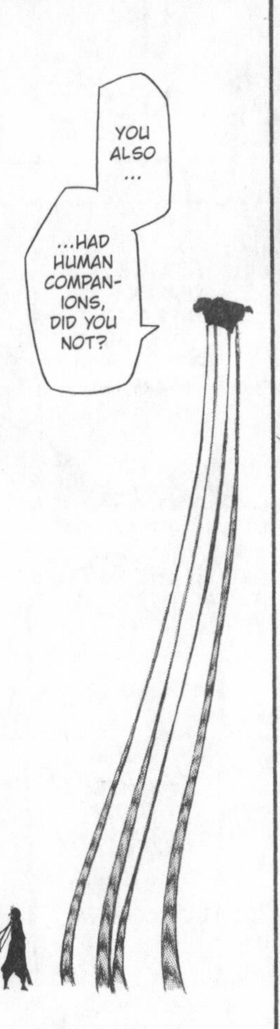
YOU ALSO ...
...HAD HUMAN COMPAN-IONS, DID YOU NOT?

HUUUH!?
AM I TALKIN' TO IMHOTEP NOW? MAN, THIS IS ANNOYING T'KEEP TRACK OF.
IF YOU HATE... ...HUMANS, THEN...
WHY DID YOU CREATE YOUR "CHURCH OF MAGAI"...??
IN ORDER TO WEAKEN FAITH IN THE GODS, AND CHIP POWER AWAY FROM THE ENNEAD?
WAS THAT REALLY IT?
"GODS CANNOT EXIST WITHOUT HUMANS."
IT IS THE SAME FOR YOU TOO.
YOU SOUGHT HUMANS WHO WOULD WORSHIP YOU.
YOU YEARNED FOR HUMANS...
...WHO WOULD NEED YOU, DIDN'T YOU?

TWITCH
HEY.
...CUT THE DELU-SIONAL CRAP.

THE PHA-RAOHS ...
...TO DEMONSTRATE THEIR AUTHORITY, THEY WOULD PRONOUNCE THEIR PERSONAL GOD TO BE THE NATIONAL GOD, AND HAVE THEIR SUBJECTS WORSHIP THAT GOD.

THE PHARAOH'S GOD WOULD STAND ABOVE ALL OF THE OTHER GODS DURING THAT REIGN.

"I WANTED TO BE CHOSEN BY A FAMOUS PHARAOH" !!!
CAN YOU HONESTLY SAY THAT FEELING HAS NOT ONCE CROSSED YOUR MIND?
ISN'T THAT WHY...
...YOU BROUGHT THOSE PHARAOHS INTO THE FOLD...!?

THE PHARAOHS? NAH, THOSE FOOLS WERE NOTHING MORE THAN GAME PIECES.
WHEN I DON'T HAVE A USE FOR 'EM ANY-MORE, I KNOCK 'EM OFF THE CHESS-BOARD.
YOU THINK I WANTED TO BE WOR-SHIPPED BY HUMANS??
HYA HA HA HA HA HA HA HA HA HA!!!
KRAK
BAM

IMHOTEP!!!
YOU'RE JUST AN IMITATION PERSON-ALITY!!
LEAP
DON'T INSULT MEEEEE!!!!
!!!?
FLASH
...THAT'S GOOD ENOUGH, MY FOOLISH SON.
IT IS COMPLETE.

THEN BEHOLD ...
...THE MOMENT IMITATIONS... WILL CHANGE THE WORLD!!

IMHOTEP FOUND!

...ARE THE FRIENDS

WAIT, WHOA !!
WHAT THE HECK IS THIS!!?
WE'RE SPARKLING ...
THE ONLY WAY TO SAVE THEM WITHOUT USING DAMNATIO MEMORIAE ...
...WAS TO LET THEM FULLY TRANSFORM INTO MAGAI...
...ABSORB THEM INTO THE MAGIC CRYSTAL, AND PURIFY THEM WITHIN IT.
HUH?
I'M...
BECAUSE ONCE THE CORRUPTION IS CLEANSED ...
...THEY CAN BE FREED FROM THE CURSE OF THE BLACK MARK.
STOP RESISTING.
Y-YOU GUUUUYS !!!
NOW THEY WILL NEVER BE CONTROLLED BY APOPHIS AGAIN!

WE CAN MAKE ...
...A SECOND STAND !!!
HYA HA HA HA HA!
DID YOU HEAR THAT, HUMANS!?
IN OTHER WORDS, THESE GUYS ABANDONED YOU ONCE ALREADY!!
FOR SOME THEORY!
YOU CAN NEVER GO BACK TO BEIN' HUMAN AGAIN!!!
YOU HATE THEM, RIGHT!!? CURSE THEM!!
GO ON!! ...
CHNK
チャキ…
YOU NEEDED TO SHOVE YOUR HAND INTO APOPHIS'S CHEST, RIGHT?

WE'RE GOING IN!!
KEEP HIM IN ONE PLACE!
ビキ
TWITCH
ビキ
TWITCH
IT'S DISSS-GUSSS-TIIING!!
FRIENDSSS!!?
WOULD YOU CALL SOMEONE YOU ABANDONED A "FRIEND"!!? ADMIT IT!! IN THE END, THEY'RE JUST BEING TURNED INTO THOTH'S PAWNSSS!!!
ビキキ
TWITCH

SUCH A FAKE WORD... I'LL DESTROY IT, DESTROY IT, DESTROY IT!!
I'LL ERASE IT AAA-AALL!!!
WHOOM
FWOOOOOO
TAM
TAM
TAM

WHACK
WHIRL
MY BAD, IMHOTEP.
I HAD TO GET ONE KICK IN!!
WHOOSH
SPLOSH
"NEITH'S CARPET"!!!
WHOA!!
TAMP

HWOOWOO

I DON'T LIKE HOW WE AIN'T ALLOWED TO CUT HIM.

RUUUMBLE

"STORM-CLOUD"!!!

RUMBLE RUMBLE RUMBLE RUMBLE RUMBLE RUMBLE RUMBLE RUMBLE

THE WORLD HAS LONG SINCE BEEN DESTROYED.

WE'VE TURNED INTO MAGAI.

WHAT'S WRONG WITH THEM......!!?

WE ALREADY HIT THE BOTTOM OF DESPAIR.

IN WHICH CASE, WE MAY AS WELL MAKE THE BEST OF OUR NEWFOUND MAGAI POWERS...

...TO TAKE YOU DOWN !!!
WHY AREN'T THEY CURSING HIM?
WHY DON'T THEY HATE HIM?
HOW ARE THEY RETAINING THEIR HUMAN FORMS?
BOOM
!!!
THIS TIME ...
... REACH HIM !!!

GUAAAH!!?
THROB

THE "BEST YOU CAN DO"...
...ISN'T ALWAYS GONNA RESULT IN THE "AWESOME RESCUE" YOU WANTED.
WHEN IT COMES TO TRAGEDY...
...REALITY IS UNFAIR.

AND THOSE PRIESTS? THEY KNOW IT TOO, APOPHIS.
THAT'S WHY THEY WON'T RESENT HIM.
BUT HE...
THAT'S THE KIND OF MAN HE IS.
...ALWAYS DID EVERYTHING IN HIS POWER TO DO THE BEST HE COULD!
IN BOTH MY ANCIENT TIME...
...AND NOW, IN HIS NEW FRIENDS' TIME.

BECAUSE THEY BELIEVE...
...IN IM.

BAM

DJOSEEER!!!

WHY?

A PHARAOH...
...IS NOT A CONQUEROR.
SHNK
GRRK
A PHARAOH IS ONE WHO PROTECTS THEIR BELOVED CHILDREN—THEIR COUNTRY.
EVEN IF I WAS DEAD...
...EGYPT STILL EXISTED IN THE PRESENT...!
I, CLEOPATRA, WILL ALLOW NO ONE TO DESTROY...
...EGYPT'S FUTURE—BE THEY MAN OR GOD!!
AS THE LAST PHARAOH OF EGYPT... I REJECT YOU!!!

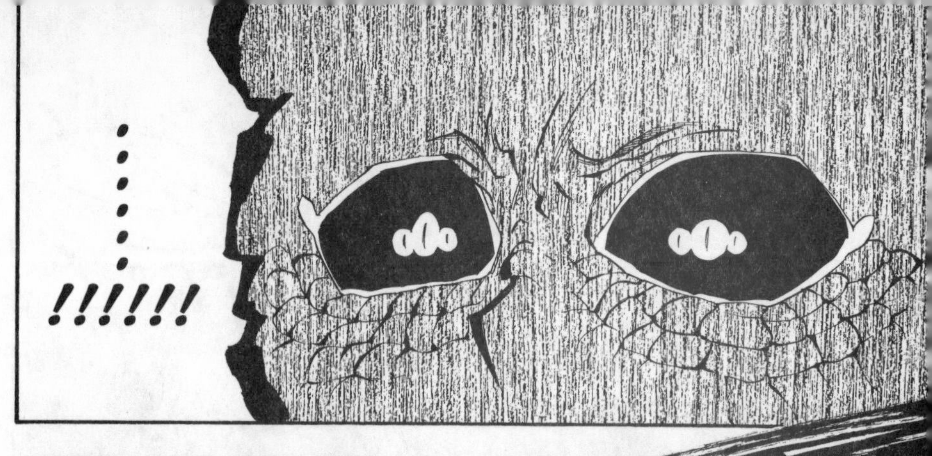

BUT I...

SSHHH

!!?

RAM-SES ...!?

PULSE PULSE PULSE PULSE PULSE PULSE PULSE

YOU'RE NOT GETTIN' AWAY!!

YOU'RE GONNA GET IN MY WAY EVEN AS A GHOST!!?

YOU DAMN DOOOO-OOG!!

DO IT! IMHOTEP !!
IMHOTEP!!
IM!
NOOOOW!!
HIT HIM!
BUT I...
GO... !!!
GO !!!
IMHOTEP!!!!

CLINK
SAVE ...
... YOUR KING !!!!

DJOSERRRRRRRR!!!!
I WAS BORN...
...IN THIS WORLD TOO!

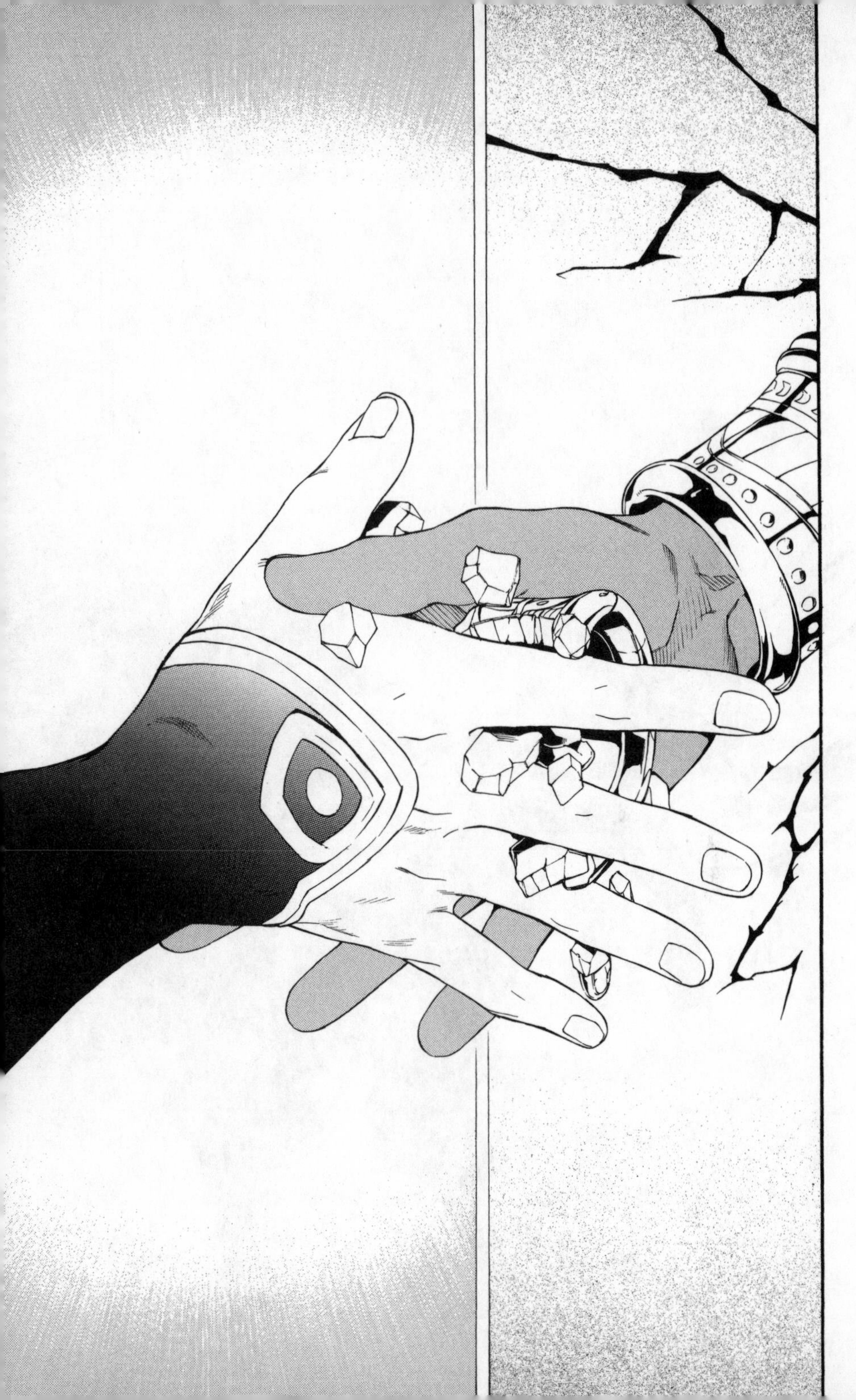

DON'T GO.

...HEH HEH HEH.

LONG TIME NO SEE...

IT'S TOO SOON...
...TO CRY.
IT AIN'T...
...OVER...YET.
IM.

Great Priest Imhotep

MASTERS...
...WHY DID YOU CREATE ME?
WHY DID YOU LEAVE ME ALIVE?

IF YOU WERE GOING TO ABANDON ME IN THE LIGHT...

...I WISH YOU HAD KILLED ME FIRST.

SCROLL 42: THE HAND THAT REACHED DAYBREAK
WE DID IT!!
NOW APOPHIS WILL BE COM- PLETELY EXPOSED ...!

SHUDDER
BWOOSH
JUST BECAUSE MY BODY ISSS GONE...
...DOESN'T MEAN YOU BRATS HAVE WON, NOW DOES IT!!?
DID YOU FORGET!?
I CAN'T DIE...! I'M THE IMMORTAL APOPHIS !!!!

DAMMIT ...NOW WHAT!!?
IMHO-TEP!! WHAT'S THE PLAN!?
!
EH... !!?
AWWW... YOU KIIILLED HIIIIM! ♪
!!?
HE'S DEAD! I DEVOURED MOST OF HIS *BA* AGES AGO.
WHAT'S MORE, HIS HEART WAS SNUFFED OUT IN HELL A LONG TIME AGO. THERE'S NOTHING OF IT LEFT.
IT SEEMS THE BOY JUST BARELY MANAGED TO ATTACH HIS *BA* TO HIS BODY USING THAT BANGLE AS AN ANCHOR...
...BUT HE DOESN'T EVEN HAVE A *KA*. HE'LL NEVER OPEN HIS EYES AGAIN!!!

IN YOUR HASTE TO RELEASE HIM FROM ME...

...YOU FINALLY FINISHED HIM OFF BY YOUR OWN HAND! HYAAAA-HA-HA-HA-HA-HA!!!

I WANT TO DIE ...!!!
DIE FOR ME ALREADY !!
SO I CAN DESTROY MY "LIFE"!
BADUM
SSS-STAY OUT OF MY WAA-AAY!
IMHOTEEEEEEP!

AHHH...

AM I GONNA DIE?

YEAAAH, I'M DYIN' HERE...

PRINCE...
...DJO...
...SER?
EH!?
EEEEEEEH!?
WHO ARE YOU-UUU!!?
HE SPO-OOO-OKE!!?
EEEEEEEH!?

YOU GOTTA GO ACK...

PLEASE MAKE UP WITH IM!!!

BWUH !!?

I-IM TOLD US...THAT HE WANTS TO MAKE UP WITH YOU!!!

NO CAN DO...
I'M ABOUT TO DIE, 'COS I DON'T HAVE A *KA*.
!!?
PLUS...
...I DON'T KNOW HOW TO APOLOGIZE AT THIS POINT ANYWAY.
WHAT I DID CAN'T BE EXCUSED WITH A REC-ONCILIATION.

WAIT, YOU'VE GOT BIGGER THINGS TO WORRY ABOUT RIGHT NOW!!
CAN YOU JUST GIVE HIM A MESSAGE FOR ME? TELL HIM I SAID, "THANKS FOR SAVING ME"!
'SCUSE ME...
BLAZE
ROOOAR
OOF !!?

BURST
CRACKLE
ULP!
WHAT WAS THAT ABOU—
!!!?
...SHE HAS NO "KA"...
HEY...
WHAT THE HELL ARE YOU THINKING...!?
...THERE IS ONE WAY...
...ONE WAY TO SAVE HER...
YOU TRANSFERRED SEKHMET TO ME!!!?
IDIOT...! YOU'RE GONNA DIE!!!!

I'LL LEND YOU MY KA... SO GO ON...!
GO TELL HIM FOR YOUR-SELF!!!
IM'S BEEN WAITING FOR YOU FOREVER!!!
IT DOESN'T HAVE TO BE AN APOLOGY.
YOU MUST HAVE TONS OF THINGS YOU REGRET NOT SAYING!!
DO YOU REALLY THINK THERE'S NOTHING YOU NEED TO SET STRAIGHT!!?
ARE YOU REALLY OKAY WITH LEAVING THINGS LIKE THIS!!?
WE WERE NEVER SUPPOSED TO BE FRIENDS, HUH...?

BY ANY CHANCE... ARE YOU... IM'S FRIEND?
THAT'S RIGHT!
HMPH!
I'M "FRIEND NUMBER TWO"!
BECAUSE OF YOU...
I'LL BE YOUR "FRIEND NUMBER ONE"!
...BOTH IM...
...AND I...
...WERE ABLE TO LEAVE OUR BOXES.
WE LEARNED TO MAKE FRIENDS ON OUR OWN!!
YOU WERE WHAT STARTED IT.

I'M GRATE-FUL...

...AND I'M PAYING BACK THE FAVOR.

I'M GONNA BORROW THIS FOR A BIT!
SKUF
THANKS, NUMBER TWO!!!

...!! AND...
...THANKS FOR ROOTIN' FOR ME!!!

BIG GUY!!

WH...!!?

WH... Y...

WE DON'T GOT MUCH TIME.
'COS IT'S BORROWED.

!!
DON'T WORRY! IF WE FINISH THIS UP FAST, SHE'S GONNA BE FINE!!

...DAMN!!

ALL RIGHT, APOPHIS.
MY PARTNER-IN-CRIME FOR THREE THOUSAND YEARS.
FOR MY LAST ACT, I'M GONNA PERFORM YOUR LAST RITES!!

IM.
LET'S GIVE THIS WORLD BACK TO THE PEOPLE OF THE PRESENT.
GRIT
AS YOU WISH, MY KING.

...AM GLAD I GOT TO BE BEST BUDS WITH YOU!!!

GRAAAAAA

"Hail be to the god of the sunrise, Ra.
"To Atum, who beautifully appears.
"Rise high, shine bright.
"The night boat vanquishes evil, the midday boat sails in good wind.
"Grant all of your power ...
"...to the pharaoh!!"
BRAAAAAH!!
IT HURTS.

IT HURTS.
I HEARD YOU.
YOU SAID, "DON'T GO."
YOUR VOICE WAS LIKE A CHILD'S.
IT HURTS.
IT WAS THE SAME AS MINE...
DON'T LEAVE ME ALL ALONE—!!!
WHY DID YOU LEAVE ME BEHIND...!?
...WHEN I WAS A LITTLE KID, STILL LOCKED UP.
THIS WHOLE TIME, YOU WERE LONELY, RIGHT?
IT WAS PAINFUL, RIGHT?
ALL YOU WANTED...
...WAS TO BE IN THE LIGHT LIKE EVERYBODY ELSE.

IT'S ALL RIGHT NOW...

...APO-PHIS.

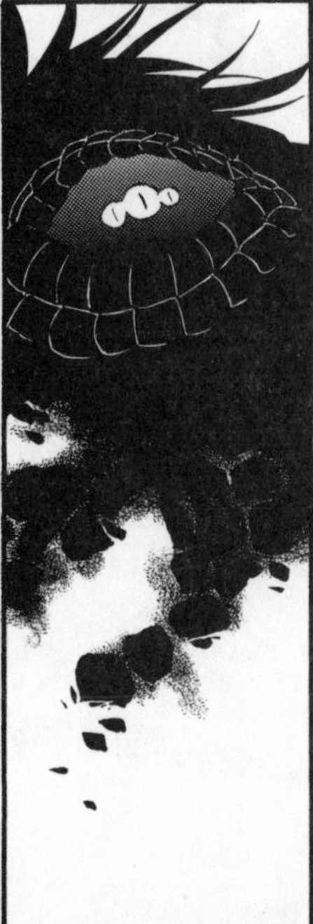

DON'T FOLLOW ...

YOU'RE ONLY...
...A STRANGER.

...AFTER ME.

PHARAOH OF THE MAGAI... ...APOPHIS.
YOU BELONG...
...IN MY PURIFI-CATION BOX.

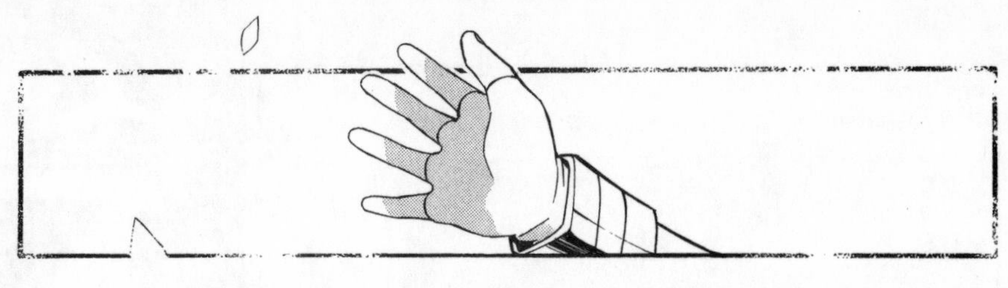

SLEEP...
...IN THE LIGHT OF THE MOON.

WHEN THIS IS ALL OVER...
...WILL YOU ALLOW ME TO WAKE YOU, MY FRIEND?

UNTIL THEN...

...SWEET DREAMS.

IS IT...
...OVER ...!?
APO-PHIS...
...IS DEAD ...?
NO.
HE'LL REVIVE AGAIN.
...NO.

...IT SEEMS HE WENT TO SLEEP ...

...IN THE LIGHT...

THUD
...... IT'S OVER ...

DID WE...
... DEFEAT HIM...?
... NOT US PRIESTS, OR THE GODS...
FLICK
THE PHARAOH DID IT.

BWUH?? MISORA, WHY ARE YOU SMOKING ??
I DUNNO. I'M SMOKING 'COS I CAN.
WHAT DO YOU SUPPOSE WE ARE NOW...??
KHONSU-SAMA.

NO...
MAGAI CULTIST... KHONSU.
YOU'RE COMING WITH US. WE'LL TAKE YOU ABOVE-GROUND.

OH YEAH. WHAT HAPPENED TO THAT WOMAN?
CLEOPATRA? DIDN'T SHE TURN BACK INTO SAND WHEN APOPHIS WAS SEALED AWAY?

NGH ...

BOLT
BUTT PILLOW
WHAT HAP-PENED !?
IS APOPHIS STILL ...!?

......

...APOPHIS... WHAT'S GONNA HAPPEN TO HIM?

HE IS NOT DEAD.
HE IS IMMORTAL, AFTER ALL.
FOR NOW, THOTH HAS PUT HIM TO SLEEP INSIDE THE MAGIC CRYSTAL.

...I SEE...

......

......
HEY, SO...
THIS MIGHT MAKE YOU MAD, BUT...
?

I...
...KNEW APOPHIS LONGER'N I KNEW YOU, DIDN'T I...?

WELL, YES...
IT WAS THREE THOUSAND YEARS.

...HIS SUF-FERING, AND...
...HIS MEMORIES AND FEELINGS AND ALL THAT... I SHARED ALL OF IT.

...I KNOW THIS IS, LIKE, UNFORGIVABLE, BUT...

ISN'T THERE... A WORLD WHERE APOPHIS WAS NEVER REJECTED...?

...WORRY NOT.
THOTH AND I CAME TO A DECISION. THE TRAGEDY THAT STRUCK APOPHIS...THE RESULTING CHAIN OF EVENTS...
...AND THE WORLD WE WENT AND DESTROYED... I WILL FIX IT ALL.

FOR IMHO-TEP...
"NOTH-ING IS IMPOS-SIBLE" !!
I KNEW I COULD COUNT ON YOU!

PFF...!
HUH!?
WHAT IS SO FUNNY ...
HFF!
HFF!
NGH!
PFFT ...
HEY...
HIC ...!!

YOU CALLED ME...YOUR "BEST BUD"...
...AGAIN... THANK...
...THANK THE GODS ...!!!!

I'M SORRY!
UHN.
HIC!
FOR LYING!
FN...
KUH ...
I'M SORRY ...
KOFF!
...I COULD NOT...
... SAVE ...Y...
HIK!
UHHN ...
UAAAGH!
NGH!
SORRY, BUD.
I MEAN IT!
UHN!
LISTEN. IM.
I KNOW ...
...YOU TRIED TO SAVE ME ON THAT FATEFUL DAY TOO...!!
THANKS FOR THAT ...!!

WITHER

...SEE YA!

...YES.

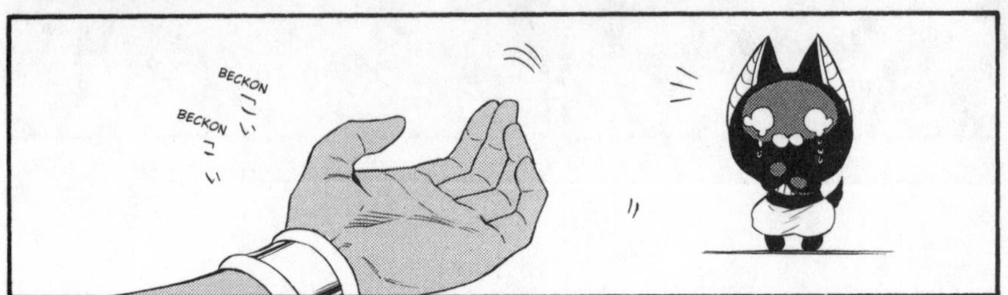
BECKON
BECKON

...LET US GO HOME...

...TO THE SURFACE.

YOU PULLED IT OFF. WELL DONE.
I HATE TO DO THIS SO SOON, BUT...

THE ENNEAD ...!!?

...HE...
...IS TO BE EXECUTED HERE AND NOW.

WHAT HE HAS DONE IS AN EVEN GREATER CRIME THAN IMHOTEP'S.
YOUR HEART WILL BE GOUGED OUT PERSONALLY BY THE ENNEAD, AND TAKEN TO THE MOUTH OF AMMIT WHILE SUFFERING ETERNAL PAIN AND AGONY.

AMMIT? WHAT'S THAT...!?

THIS IS HORRIBLE...! THAT'S THE MONSTER WHO DEVOURS THE HEARTS OF CRIMINALS ...!!

WAIT!! LET US SPEAK FIRST!!

KHONSU IS ATUM'S ...!!

IF YOU'RE GONNA KILL ME ANYWAY...

...THAT MEANS I CAN DO ANYTHING, EVEN THE MOST PROFANE OF ACTS...!

FWOOSH

ATUM-
SAMA-
AA!!!
GRAB

YOU SURE HAVE GROWN ...
... "SHAMS."

FILTHY!
BACK OFF, CRIMINAL!!!
......
!!?
WH...
HE'S ...!

PATIENT DATA: FORMER HIGH PRIEST KHONSU
MARK PROGRESSION: END-STAGE
...THOSE JUDGED "GUILTY" BY THE CASTER ARE TORN APART.
MAGIC DATA: ARGYROS SER (COURT OF THE SILVER MOON)
...THOSE JUDGED "NOT GUILTY" BY THE CASTER HAVE THEIR WOUNDS ERASED.
HIS THEFT OF PHARAOH DJOSER'S MUMMY...
...AND HIS CLEAR BETRAYAL OF THE PRIESTHOOD FOR THE MAGAI CULT DEVASTATED THE WORLD.
ON AUGUST 21, HE DIED A NATURAL DEATH.
RECORDED BY HIGH PRIEST HESIRE.

THE ETERNAL BATTLE...

...ENDED ONCE AGAIN.

BUT THERE'S STILL...

...MUCH TO DO.

WILL THE WORLD END, OR CONTINUE?

THE DECISION WAS ENTRUSTED TO THOTH.

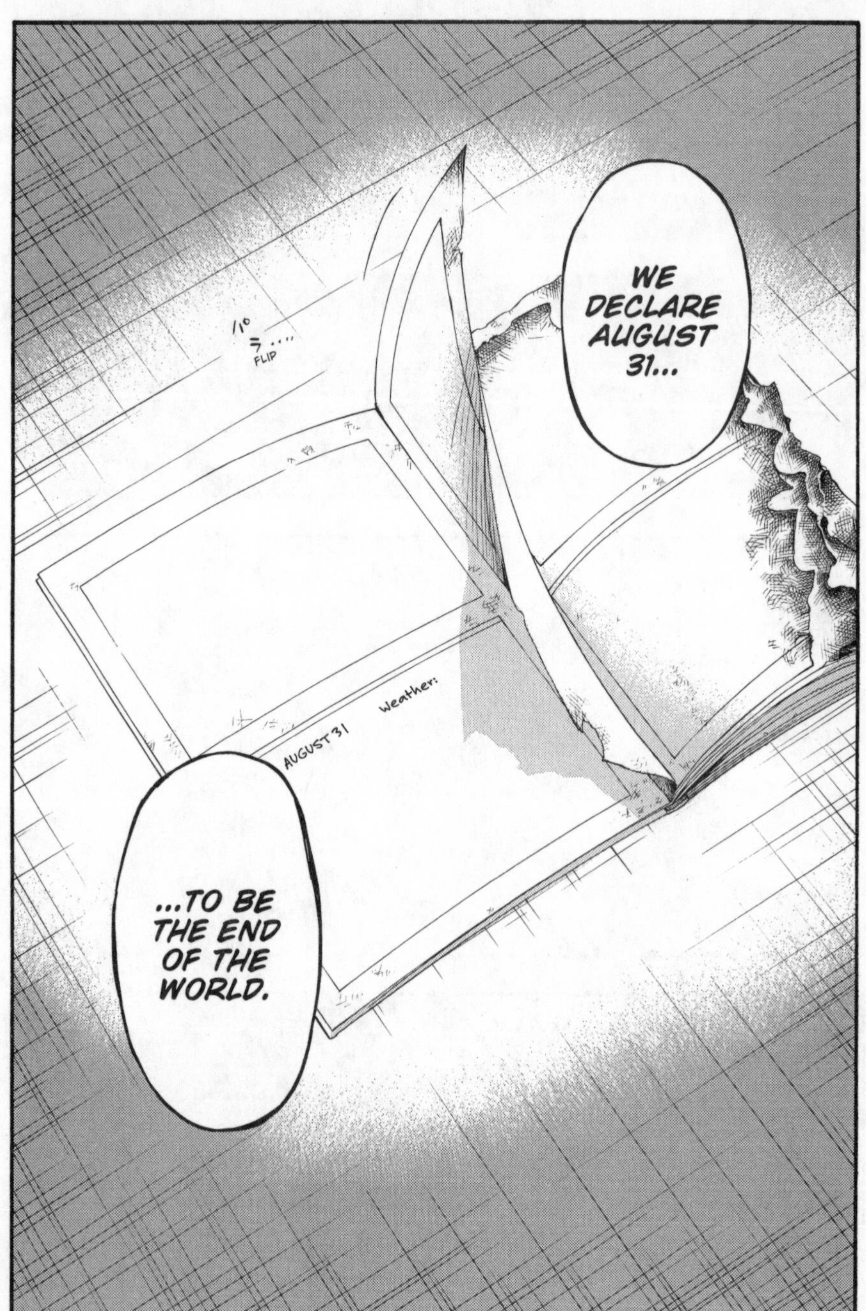
WE DECLARE AUGUST 31...
FLIP
AUGUST 31
Weather:
...TO BE THE END OF THE WORLD.

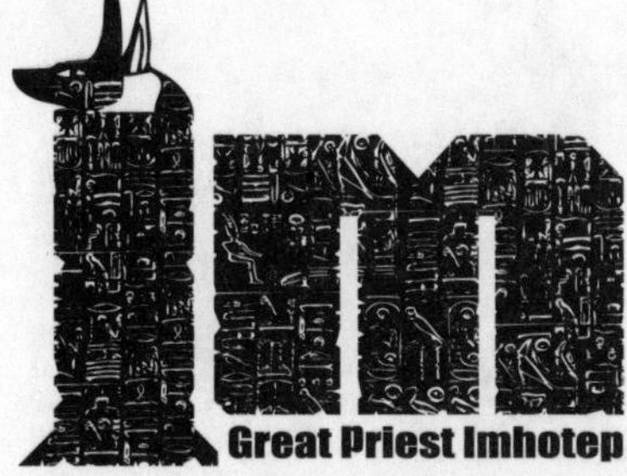
Great Priest Imhotep

Great Priest Imhotep

MORNING, HINOME-CHAN!!
MORNING, KOBUSHI!
AH!!
YOU TANNED A LITTLE!
DID YOU HAVE FUN ON YOUR TRIP TO EGYPT??
UMM...
THAT'S KIND OF A LONG STORY...
I'LL TELL YOU LITTLE BY LITTLE...
DO NOT LEAVE ME BEHIND!!
WAIIIT!!
ANYWAY, HERE! I GOT YOU A SOUVE-NIR...
VROOOOM
AH!!
WHOMP

FINAL SCROLL: I'M...

Great Priest Imhotep

SEPTEMBER 1

AHEM...

FIRST OF ALL... I'M PLEASED TO SEE THAT NONE OF YOU HAVE GOTTEN INTO TROUBLE AND YOU'RE ALL BACK IN CLASS. (STRAIGHT FROM THE SCRIPT)

I DIDN'T GET ANY NEWS ABOUT ANYONE GETTING BADLY HURT OVER SUMMER VACATION EITHER.

CLASS 1-3

BUT YOU KNOW ...

...I NEVER SAID YOU COULD GO GETTING HURT ONCE YOUR VACATION ENDED!

WHISPER
ON THE FIRST DAY BACK ...?
WHISPER
THE HAWAKATAS REALLY ARE CURSED.
WHISPER
BAM
AGH!
CRACK
GYAAAH!
THROB
THROB
IDIOT IMMM... HOW MANY TIMES HAVE I TOLD YOU TO LOOK BOTH WAYS FOR CARS BEFORE YOU CROSS THE STREET!!?
KACLINK
LEARN YOUR LESSON!

SENSEI!!
FWAP
HINOME DID NOT DO HER HOMEWORK HERSELF. I DID MOST OF IT!!
SO SHE DOES NOT NEED THESE "KREHD-IT" THINGS.
THIS IS MATH, THIS IS PHYSICS, AND OH, DO THIS TOO...
YOU SNITCH!!!?

THERE WAS NO WAY I COULD DO MY HOMEWORK IN THOSE CIRCUMSTANCES!!!
GYARGH!
EXCUSES!
WHY IS THAT BOY HERE AGAIN ...?
OUR TUMULTUOUS SUMMER VACATION ENDED...
ALL RIGHT. HAND IN YOUR PICTURE DIARIES.
...AND WE RETURNED HOME TO JAPAN SAFE AND SOUND.

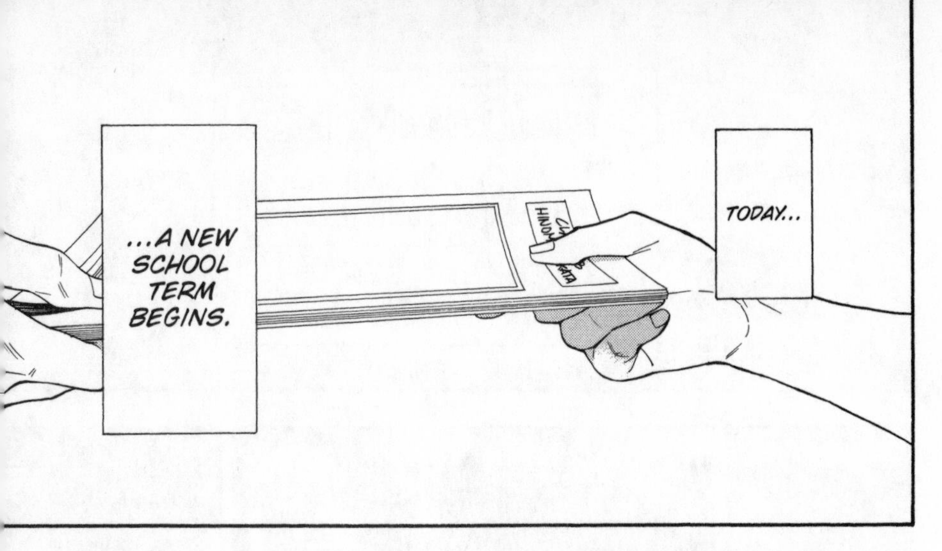
TODAY...
...A NEW SCHOOL TERM BEGINS.

WHAT!!?
THERE ARE NO LESSONS TODAY!?
DUH! TODAY'S ONLY THE OPENING CEREMONY!
HAWAKATA!! YOU DIDN'T TURN IN YOUR FUTURE PLANS SURVEY FIRST TERM.
I WANT IT BEFORE YOU LEAVE TODAY!

DID YOU DECIDE...
...ON YOUR FUTURE PLANS?
YUP!

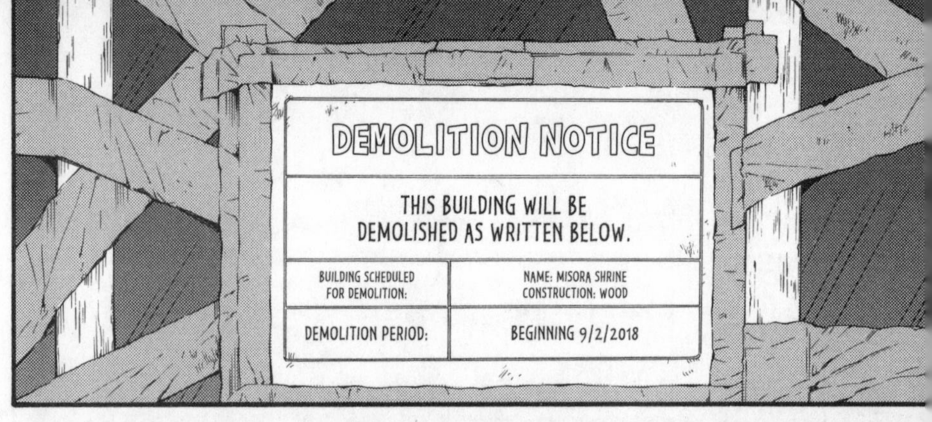
DEMOLITION NOTICE
THIS BUILDING WILL BE DEMOLISHED AS WRITTEN BELOW.
BUILDING SCHEDULED FOR DEMOLITION:
NAME: MISORA SHRINE
CONSTRUCTION: WOOD
DEMOLITION PERIOD:
BEGINNING 9/2/2018

HEY...
CLATTER
KRAK
KRAK
...YOU SURE IT'S OKAY TO COME IN HERE!?
I MEAN, YOU KNOW... ISN'T THIS PLACE...LIKE... WHERE YOU... Y'KNOW...?
OKAY, I'LL JUST COME OUT AND SAY IT!!! THIS IS TOTALLY NUTS, MAN!!! LET'S GET OUTTA HERE!! WE'RE GONNA GET IN TROUBLE FROM ALL SIDES!!!
CLINK
CLINK
LIKE I CARE.
CLACK
RATTLE
THIS IS MY HOUSE.
CLICK

SPLAT

...UH.
THIS IS DEFINITELY WRONG.
CLUNK
SHUT UP AND CUT THE OCTOPUS, DUMMY-NABA.
CLUNK
NO, DON'T YOU BOIL IT FIRST?
SHK
SHK
SHK
SHK

THIS IS IMHO-TEP'S GOING-AWAY PARTY, RIGHT!?
I EVEN WENT FISHING THROUGH THE FOOD BLOGS TO FIND A NICE RESTAURANT TO GET A RESERVATION AT!!!
SQUABBLE
SQUABBLE
SO WHY...
...DID WE END UP GOING WITH A TAKOYAKI PARTY AT YOUR HOUSE!!?
THE GUEST OF HONOR WAS ALL FOR IT.
IF YOU ACTUALLY THOUGHT ABOUT IT, YOU'D HAFTA BE CRAZY TO PICK THIS PLACE FOR A PAR—
WHACK
OW !!!
LOW VISCOSITY WHEAT FLOUR
YAKI SAUCE!

YOU SURE ARE NOISY, NII-CHAN!
QUIT COMPLAININ' AN' HELP!

WE MIXED THE BATTER.
ALMOST READY.
OKAY, IT'S SERIOUSLY EMBARRASSING TO GET TOLD OFF BY A CHILD I'VE NEVER EVEN MET BEFORE!

ガララララ
RATTLE
WE ARE HEEERE !!
HEY! MIND YOUR MAN-NERS!!
ぱ
FLING
IT HAS BEEN TOO LONG, RYUUUU!!
RYUU-KUN!

IMHOTEP-NIICHAAAN !!
AND HIS DOG!!
M...MAY WE COME IN?
AH!! HINO... OLD CAT'S CRADLE HAG! LONG TIME NO SEE!!
WHY DID YOU CORRECT YOURSELF !!?

SLIIIIDE
YAHOOO-OOOOOO-OOOOO!!!
SO THIS IS "GOING OVER TO A FRIEND'S HOUSE"! I'VE ALWAYS WANTED TO DO THIS!!
THAT'S GONNA MESS UP THE FLOOR!!! CUT IT OUT OR YOU'RE DEAD MEAT!!!
SCARY...
TWIRL
AHHH! HIMEKO-CHAN, IS THAT A SCHOOL UNIFORM!!?
I'M GOING TO AN ORDINARY MIDDLE SCHOOL AS OF THIS TERM!
IT'S MY BIG UNIFORM REVEAL!

SPEAKING OF SCHOOL, INABA-DONO BECAME A TEACHER FOR THE ORPHANS IN CROW'S BROOD.
AND MISORA-DONO SAYS HE WANTS TO GO TO COLLEGE!
WE AREN'T PRIESTS ANYMORE, AFTER ALL.
OH MY GOSH!!
SEE!? IT SAYS TO BOIL IT FIRST!!
OKAY, KEEP STILL.
PUT THE KNIFE DOWN!!
SO YOU'RE ALL STARTING DOWN NEW PATHS!!

YOU TRULY MADE AN EXCELLENT DOG, SED.

SO EXCELLENT... THAT IT CAME BACK TO BITE ME.

LISTEN.
USE THAT BLOODIED BODY TO GIVE HQ A MESSAGE— "KHONSU MADE OFF WITH THE MUMMY."
DON'T FAIL ME.
!?
I NO LONGER HAVE A CHANCE OF WINNING FROM THIS SIDE.
SO I'LL LEAVE IT.
THAT'S REASON ENOUGH, NO?
...IT DOESN'T MATTER TO ME ANYWAY.
AS LONG AS I CAN RELEASE MY LITTLE BROTHER FROM THE GODS...
...I DON'T CARE IF THE WORLD ENDS.
...BUT...
...HE WON'T STOP NAGGING ME.

IT LOOKS LIKE... FOR "KHONSU"... FRIENDS WERE MORE IMPORTANT THAN I THOUGHT.
I WON'T BE ABLE TO FULLY BECOME YOUR ENEMY LIKE THIS, WILL I?
SO I'LL GIVE YOU...
...ONE LAST ORDER AS "PRIEST KHONSU."
TUG
......!!!
SNAP
...COULD YOU GO CALL THE SAVIOR IMHOTEP FOR ME...?
SO THE PEOPLE WHO CARED ABOUT KHONSU ...
...EVEN IF JUST ONE... CAN SURVIVE THIS.

KHONSU IS DEAD NOW.
YOU WON'T NEED THAT COLLAR ANYMORE.
I'M LETTING YOU GO.
CIAO.
AH.
SORRY, SHAMS-KUN. OLD HABITS.
NO, IT'S OKAY.
...YOU BIG BUF-FOON.

BECAUSE HE REALLY WAS A BIG BUFFOON.

SHOULD I ENGRAVE "BIG BUFFOON" ON HIS GRAVE-STONE?
NO, NO, NO.

WHEN WE LIVED IN THAT OLD, RAMSHACKLE HOUSE, NII-SAN NEVER LET ME GO OUTSIDE.
...SO I NEVER HEARD... WHAT OTHER PEOPLE CALLED HIM.

EVEN THOUGH WE'RE FAMILY...
...I COULDN'T REMEMBER HIS NAME FOR HIM.

...I'M AN AWFUL LITTLE BROTHER, AREN'T I?

YOUR BIG BROTHER LEFT YOU BEHIND THE MOMENT AFTER YOU FOUND EACH OTHER. HE'S NOT ANY BETTER.
HMPH!
I THINK YOU'RE EVEN.

THANK YOU FOR ARRANGING THIS FUNERAL FOR NII-SAN...

...AUSIR-SAN.

...I HONOR ALL THE DEAD EQUALLY. DON'T READ INTO IT.
THEEERE YA GO AGAAAIN!!!
NWOOP にょきっ

Y'EVEN SECRETLY MADE HIM A GRAVE INSIDE OUR ESTATE SO HQ WON'T FIND OUT!!!
REALLY, M'LORD, WHAT'S GOTTEN INTO YOU!!?
SPEAKIN' OF!! ARE YOU REALLY TALKIN' TO YUUTO-SAMA EXTRA-RESPECT-FULLY!!?
HAPI... GO BACK TO JAIL.

YUU-TOOO!!! WAIT FOR MEEE!!
ドサーッ
WHUMP
WHAAAT!? HOW COULD YOUUUU!!!

HAHAHAHAHA!
GYAHAHAHAHAHAHA
UNCLE! UNCLE! UNCLE!!
HEEELP!!!
THIS KID HASN'T CHANGED INSIDE AT AAAALL!!!
THOSE KIDS...
...MUST BE EXCITED TO HAVE A FRIEND CLOSE TO THEIR AGE FOR THE FIRST TIME.
LOOKS LIKE SETH HAD A BIG INFLUENCE ON THE KID'S PERSONALITY DEVELOPMENT......

ALL THE VESSELS WERE FREED...
...AND THE GODS WILL LEAVE THIS WORLD SOON TOO.
WE HAVE TO THINK ABOUT HOW WE'LL LIVE IN THE NEW, CHANGING WORLD TOO.
ABOUT THE PATHS WE'LL WALK.

FOR US WHO'VE LIVED OUR WHOLE LIVES IN SERVICE TO THE GODS...
... "FREEDOM" MIGHT BECOME A NEW AGONY.
OUR PATHS MAY TAKE ...
...DIFFERENT DIRECTIONS. EVEN SO...
...LET'S LIVE, TOGETHER.
FOR THE SAKE OF THOSE WHO'LL COME AFTER US...THE PEOPLE OF THE FUTURE WE'VE YET TO SEE.
BY YOUR WILL!
OLD HABITS DIE HAAARD!!
I COMPLETELY THOUGHT YA WERE ATUM-SAMA THERE!!
CACKLE
CACKLE
HE GETS HIS LAUGH FROM KHON-KHON...
UNTIL WE MEET AGAIN ...
... KHONSU-NIISAN.

TARS
STONE MARKT
CE
HOOOOOHOHOHO! ♡
AHHH, WHAT FUN! ♪ I WISH TO EAT "SWEETS" NEXT!!! TAKE ME TO THEM. ♡
Ga
BRADA

CLEO-PATRA !!
WHY DIDN'T YOU DISAP-PEAR...
...WHEN APOPHIS WAS DEFEATED !!?
OH, IT WAS A SURPRISE FOR ME TOO.
SO I THOUGHT I MAY AS WELL HAVE THE TIME OF MY LIFE IN MODERN EGYPT WHILE I HAVE THE CHANCE!!

I'M SURE I'LL RETURN TO DIRT ANY MOMENT NOW.
GO ALONG WITH YOUR FELLOW WOMAN'S FUN, WON'T YOU, DEAR? FOR ONE LAST HURRAH?

THERE'S NO TIME TO BE DOWN IN THE DUMPS, LATO.
...!!

RAM-SES AND I...
DJO-SER... IMHO-TEP...
WE SHALL DEPART, AND THIS TIME, BECOME RELICS OF THE PAST FOR GOOD.

PROTECT OUR HOME-LAND, OUR EGYPT, IN THE NEW WORLD.
EVEN IF YOU NO LONGER HAVE YOUR DUTIES. EVEN IF THERE ARE NO GODS.
ALL RIGHT?

I WON'T LET IT BE DES-TROY-ED.
NOT BY ANY-ONE.

OH! WE HAVE TO ORDER AT THE COUNTER HERE.
ARE YOU OKAY WITH ANY-THING? I'LL GO DO IT.

......THANK YOU.

CLATTER
カタン

24h OPEN!
DISCOUNT PALACE DON QUIXOTE
MARUSAN
WELP, GUESS IT'S ABOUT TIME TO DISBAND!!
DISCOUNT PALACE DON QUIXOTE
DISCOUNT PALACE DON QUIXOTE

NEED ANY SCORE SHEETS?

17:28
September 1
Upload Data
84%
NEW M
Did you have fun?

I'LL WALK RYUU-KUN TO THE STATION.
WE'D GO IN THE SAME DIRECTION ANYWAY.
YOU SURE?
UH-HUH!
THANKS FOR TODAY, IM-KUN!!
TAKE CARE!
BYE!!

HARUGO... WEREN'T YOU GOING TO CUT ME DOWN?
DON'T HAVE THE KATANA ANYMORE.
THE CHAPTER CHIEF TOOK IT.
...I'M SURPRISED YOU WELCOMED ME INTO YOUR SHRINE TODAY.
THE *KID WHO USED THAT ROOM* DIDN'T LOSE HIS LIFE... SO LET'S JUST SAY HIS ROOM IS A SPECIAL ZONE.

IT WAS MY FIRST TIME HAVIN' FRIENDS IN THERE TOO.

CHOP
どすっ

LEAVE THE NEW FUTURE TO US PEOPLE OF THE PRESENT.

I'M COUNT-ING ON YOU.
I LEAVE IT IN YOUR HANDS.

EVERYONE... I OWE YOU, TRULY!! THANK YOU!!
AND FAREWELL !!!

THAT WAS FUN.

YEAH ...

......BY THE BY, HINOME.
WHAT DID YOU END UP CHOOSING FOR YOUR FUTURE PLANS?

I-I'M NOT TELLING.
I MEAN... I DON'T KNOW WHETHER IT'LL COME TRUE... AND I'LL BE SO EMBAR-RASSED IF IT DOESN'T...

I SEE.
IT'S THAT GOOD OF A DREAM, IS IT?

...IM.
I'M GONNA GO HOME FIRST, 'KAY?
TEP
TEP
TEP
TEP
HUH?

ONEE-CHAN...!!!

THANKS A WHOLE, WHOLE LOT...!!!

STAY WELL!!

YOU MIGHT... FORGET ABOUT ME...

...BUT DON'T FORGET, OKAY!!?

I WON'T FORGET!!!

DASH
ANUBIS !!? WHAT ARE YOU TALKING ABOUT ...!?
WAIT !!!
17:59
September 1
NEW MESSAGE
It's done.
Upload Data
100%
...IT IS TIME.

RUSTLE
DO YOU REMEMBER?
AHHH... YEAH.
YEAH, I REMEMBER NOW.
TODAY'S *REAL DATE* IS...

...AUGUST 31.
IT WAS...
...STILL SUMMER VACATION.
AUGUST 31
Weather:
Today is the last day. I'm remembering that festival night. That was the night I knew, I think.
I knew that this summer vacation would be my first and last summer vacation with my friend who'd crossed the sands of time.

APOPHIS...
...ENDED COUNTLESS LIVES.
"IN THE NEAR FUTURE, THE WORLD WILL END."
THAT IS WHY...
...IT WAS DECIDED THOTH AND I WOULD USE DAMNATIO MEMORIAE TO RECONSTRUCT THE WORLD.
WE WOULD ERASE ONLY "THE EXISTENCE OF GODS" FROM HISTORY'S RECORDS, CREATING *A WORLD ADVANCED ONLY BY HUMANS*.
WHILE WE SPENT THIS DAY TOGETH-ER...
...THOTH COMPLETED THE UPDATE TO THE NEW WORLD.
HE SPOKE TO ME LIKE A FATHER. "I'LL HANDLE THE REST MYSELF. YOU GO HAVE FUN."
ONCE THIS FICTIONAL SEPTEMBER 1ST DISAPPEARS...
...THE NEW WORLD, ONE WITHOUT GODS, WILL BEGIN.

...WHAT ABOUT EVERYONE WHO WAS WITH US TODAY?

THEY WERE ALL THEIR TRUE SOULS.
WORRY NOT. THEY WILL BE IN THE RECON-STRUCTED WORLD TOO.

BUT...
...BECAUSE THE "GODS" THAT CONNECTED US WILL BE GONE...
...MANY OF THEM WILL HAVE BECOME COMPLETE STRANGERS.

AND EVEN WITH THE GODS GONE...
...DEPENDING ON THE PERSON, THEIR FATES, THEIR HISTORY, WILL NOT CHANGE.

...CALL IT SELFISH IF YOU WISH.
WE THOUGHT THIS WAS THE BEST WAY TO SAVE THIS WORLD FROM RUIN.

WE WILL NOT ALLOW EVEN THE OGDOAD TO TOUCH IT.
I VOW TO PROTECT YOU ALL ETERNALLY.

I WON'T BLAME YOU.

WE DECIDED IT WAS FOR THE BEST TOGETHER, DIDN'T WE?

YOU ASKED US WHAT WE THOUGHT TOO.

THANK YOU. FOR CARING ABOUT US ALL SO MUCH.

...TO SPEND THIS FINAL DAY...

...WITH YOU, MY FRIENDS... AS A "NORMAL KID."

SHATTER
IT SEEMS THIS IS GOOD-BYE.
......AH!!!
HUH!?
THERE IS ONE MORE IMPORTANT THING I MUST TELL YOU!!
WHA!!?
WHAT IS IT!? SOMETHING BIG!? IS THE WORLD STILL IN DANGER!?
ENOUGH ALREADY!!
IT'S SOMETHING I'D HAVE TERRIBLY REGRETTED NOT TELLING YOU!!!
TODAY IS AUGUST 31!!

HINOME.
HAPPY BIRTHDAY!!!

...DON'T MAKE ME CRY ...!!!

HM?

AH!

MEETING YOU...AND ANUBIS...

...WAS SO MUCH FUN!!

WE'RE FRIENDS...

...BUT MORE THAN THAT...!!

NO...

I DON'T WANT TO FORGET YOU...!!!

YOU WERE LIKE FAMILY ...!!!

ICE

POTATO

THOUGH I'LL PASS...

...ON HAVING ANYONE AS DIFFI-CULT AS YOU AGAIN ...!

SCRUB

ごしっ

IM...

I'LL BE OKAY NOW!!

THANK YOU...
...FOR BEING FRIENDS WITH ME...
...IN THIS TIME... !!!!
SAME HERE.
THANKS FOR BECOMING FRIENDS WITH ME!!
I LOVE YOU!!!

MY DREAM...
I'M GONNA MAKE IT COME TRUE!!

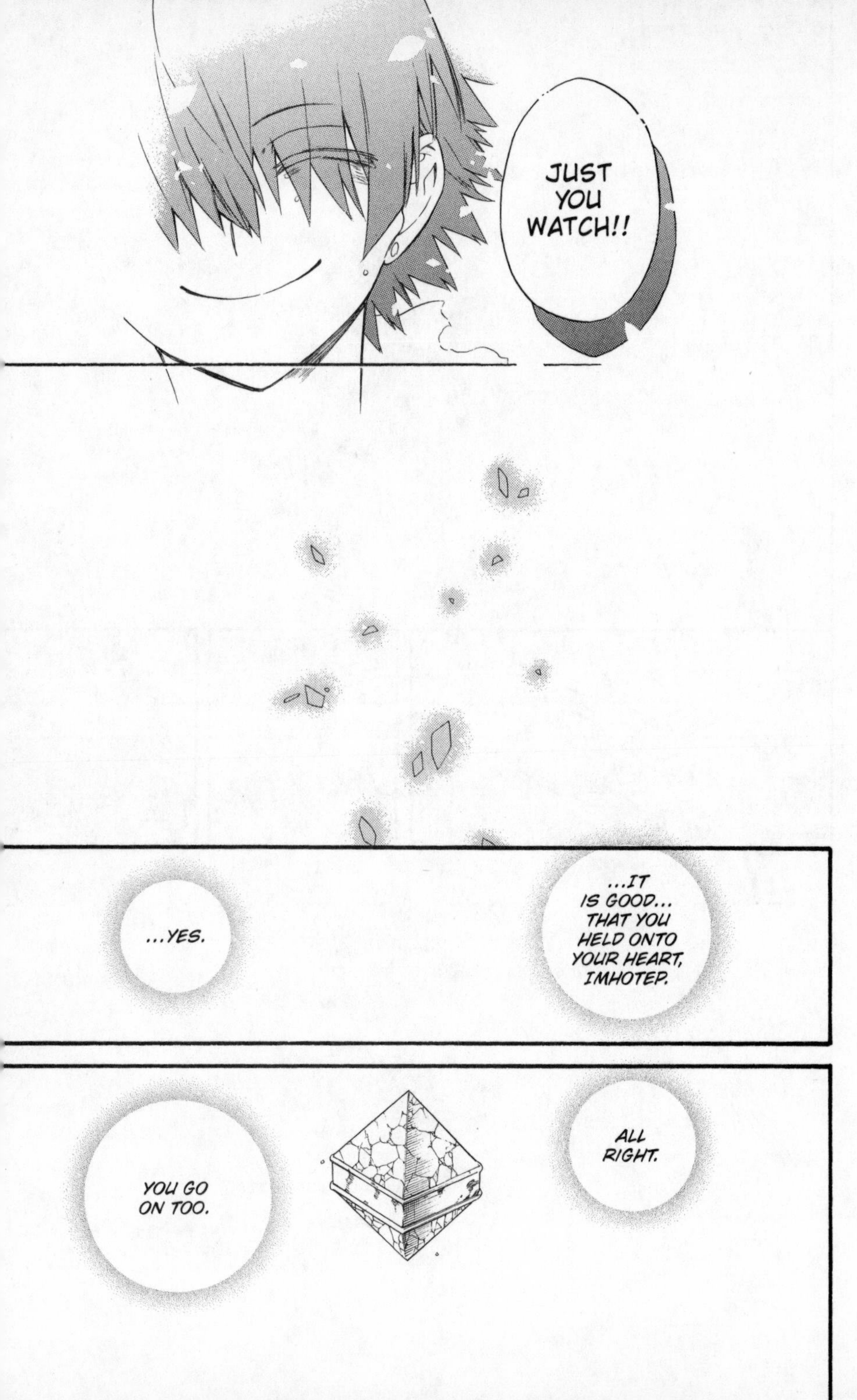
JUST YOU WATCH!!
...IT IS GOOD... THAT YOU HELD ONTO YOUR HEART, IMHOTEP.
...YES.
ALL RIGHT.
YOU GO ON TOO.

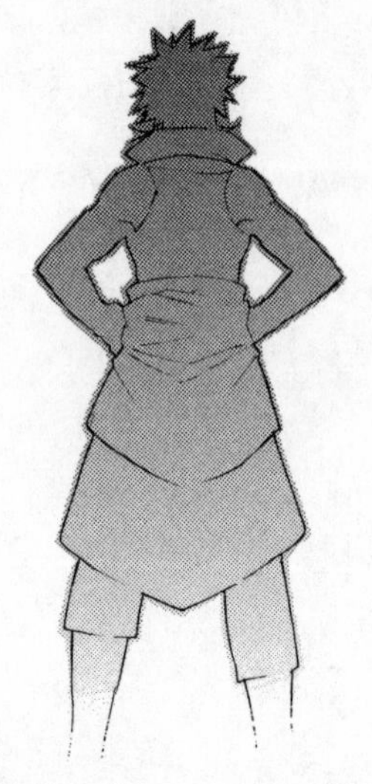

WELL DONE.

ROARRRR
CAIRO INTERNATIONAL AIRPORT
TERMINAL 1

Mysterious Giant Pyramid Appears!!!!
NEW DISCOVERY!!
Possibly the oldest!?
"THE SUDDEN APPEARANCE OF A MYSTERIOUS GIANT PYRAMID."

...THAT CAN'T BE POSSIBLE...
NATIONAL NEWS
HINOME-CHAN, GRAB THE LUG-GAGE!!

WILL YOU STOP USING "-CHAN"!?
I'M TWENTY YEARS OLD!!
EEK!!

MORE IMPORTANTLY, WHY DID YOU SUDDENLY DECIDE TO COME WITH ME!?
YOU WERE NEVER INTERESTED IN EGYPT BEFORE!

NO REAL REASON.

I JUST FELT LIKE IT.

UMMM, OUR GUIDE SHOULD BE...

WHUUUH!!?

MY LUNCH IS JUST BREAD AGAIN TODAY!!?

VROOOM
WOW! SO YOUR DAUGHTER WRITES PICTURE BOOKS!!
AND FOR HER FIRST TIME IN EGYPT, SHE GETS TO SEE THAT PYRAMID?
THAT'S GONNA MAKE A PRETTY BIG IMPRES-SION!

THEY DON'T EVEN KNOW THE PHA-RAOH'S NAME YET.
THIS STEP PYRAMID IS COMPLETELY UNIDENTIFIED.

I'VE LIVED IN EGYPT ALL MY LIFE.
I CAN'T BELIEVE I NEVER NOTICED THIS HUGE THING UNTIL JUST RECENTLY. IT'S CRAZY, RIGHT?
OHH, IT'S SO MYSTE-RIOUS!
TIIING
TIIING
VOICES ...?
BOY, THAT'S HUGE.
IT IS ALMOST COMPLETE.
I HAVE A FEELING I WANTED TO BUILD THIS FOR A VERY LONG TIME.
MY TOMB??
THAT IS NOT TO SAY THAT I WISH YOU WOULD HURRY TO DIE...
I KNOW, I KNOW!!
... HUH? WHAT ...?
ARE YOU CRYING?

WITH JOY.
...WELP.
IT'S THE ROYAL TOMB MY GREAT VIZIER BUILT FOR ME.
WHEN I END UP IN THERE, REGARDLESS OF HOW I MET MY END...
...I BET I'LL BE ABLE TO SAY...
..."THAT WAS ONE AWESOME LIFE."

ぎょっ
JOLT
!!?
WHAT'S THE MATTER!? ARE YOU THAT MOVED?

I DON'T KNOW ...
... BUT ...
...... RIGHT NOW... I REALLY ......!

... REALLY WANNA SAY...
... "GOOD FOR YOU" ...!!!

TITLE: "I'M" (I AM)

ONCE UPON A TIME...
...A BOY WHO USED TO BE ALL ALONE...
... WORRIED FOR HIS PRECIOUS FRIEND...
...STOOD UP TO FIGHT...
...AND CAUSED A MIRACLE. AN ADVENTURE STORY.

THE PEOPLE WHO KNOW...

...THE NAME THAT COMES AFTER "I'M"...

...ARE SOMEWHERE OUT IN THE WORLD.
I'VE GOT THAT FEELING.

I'm

Hinome Hawakata

"I'M...
...
IMHÖTEP."

Thank you for reading!

TO PURIFY THE EVIL IN THE WORLD...

...THEY WOULD EXILE CRIMINALS THROUGH A DOOR THEY CALLED "HELL'S GATE."

ONCE EVERY FEW HUNDRED YEARS...

...THEY WOULD OFFER UP THE HEART OF A **PRINCE WITH A SPECIAL SOUL** AS A SACRIFICE.

THE SUN PRINCE IS KEPT CONFINED IN THE ROYAL PALACE...
...FOR HE IS A VERY IMPORTANT SACRIFICE.
YES.
HE WOULDN'T BE IN A PLACE LIKE THIS.
THE PRE-CIOUS PRINCE COULD NEVER BE HUNG UP IN THE WASTE-LANDS ......

HEEEEELP!!!!

SIDE SCROLL: PRINCE DJOSER'S
EGYPTIAN CASE FILES

IT ALL BEGAN ...
...IN KARNAK, THE PALACE TOWN.
A VILLAGE WITH NO WATER AT ALL!!?
KHASEKHEMWY'S SECOND SON DJOSER (SUN PRINCE)
THAT'S RIGHT. WE PASS THROUGH THIS VILLAGE WHEN WE TRANSPORT THINGS.
EVERY TIME WE GO THERE, IT'S DRY AS A BONE!
IT'S IN THE MIDDLE OF NOWHERE, SO YOU PROBABLY DON'T KNOW IT.
THE NILE FLOODS EVERY YEAR, YET SOMEHOW THAT LONE VILLAGE ...
...HAS BEEN PLAGUED BY DROUGHT FOR SEVERAL YEARS NOW!
AND THEY SAY NEITHER THE ROYAL FAMILY NOR THE PRIESTHOOD HAS SENT ANY HELP...
WHAT !!?

WHAT THE HECK IS MY OLD MAN DOING!!?
PRINCE, WHERE ARE YOU GOING!?
I'M GONNA GO CHECK OUT THAT VILLAGE!!
ZOOM
PRINCE, UM...WHAT ABOUT YOUR BILL!?
THAT IS MAD!
PUT IT ON MY TAB!!!
BETTER DISGUISE MYSELF...
AND SO I RUSHED OFF WITHOUT A SECOND THOUGHT...
ZSSHHH
BUT IT WAS MY FIRST TIME OUT-SIDE OF THE CITY.
SO I NEVER WOULDA KNOWN HOW HARSH THE DESERT IS...
NEXT THING I KNEW ...
...I'D ENDED UP LIKE THIS.

LOOK AT HIS BELONGINGS!!
THEY'RE ALL GOLD!!!
THAT PROVES IT... THEN HE REALLY IS A...
...BANDIT!!!
NO, I'M A PRIIINCE!!!
WHAT IS THERE TO STEAL IN A VILLAGE LIKE OURS!?
WE HAVE BARELY ANY MONEY TO SPEAK OF!
WHAT WE WANT IS WATER, NOT MONEY!!!
AHA...
FOR BETTER OR WORSE, I MADE IT TO THE VILLAGE I WAS LOOKING FOR...
GIVE US FOOD!!!
IF YOU DON'T, WE'LL TAKE A BITE OUT OF YOU!!
EEK!!!

BESIDES, WE'VE NEVER HEARD OF A PRINCE NAMED "DJOSER"!

THERE'S ONLY ONE PRINCE—SANAKHT!

PRETENDING TO BE A ROYAL? SHAME ON YOUUU!!

THUNK

SO OUT IN THE COUNTRY, THEY DON'T EVEN KNOW THE YOUNGER PRINCE EXISTS!?

BET THIS IS 'COS MY OLD MAN WAS KEEPIN' ME INSIDE TOO!!

TSK! HE'S USELESS.

DO WE BURY HIM?

NOOOO!!

WHAT ARE YOU DOING!!?

VILLAGE CHIEF!
STOP YOUR FOOLISHNESS AT ONCE!
A GREAT PRIEST HAS GRACED US WITH HIS PRESENCE !!!
BAM
GASP
ざわ…
A GREAT PRIEST ...!!?
OHH ...
A GOD HAS COME TO SAVE US...!!
IMMM!!!
IT'S IMHOTEEEP !!!

MURMUR

HELP MEEE !!!

IGNORED

WHY!!?

WE'RE FRIENDS, RIGHT!!?

(*SEE SCROLL 6)

A MOMENT AGO, I HEARD THE WORDS "BURY HIM" ...

IS THAT NOT TANTAMOUNT TO MURDER?

HE'S "HELL'S GATE-KEEPER."

WHISPER

OF ALL PEOPLE, IT HAD TO BE HIM...!!?

WHISPER

I HEARD HE EVEN CAST A LITTLE CHILD WHO BEGGED FOR FORGIVENESS FOR THEIR PRANK INTO HELL... HE SHOWS NO MERCY...

HE'S TERRI-FYING!

WHISPER

OHH... HAVE THE GODS FORSAKEN US...?

ALLOW US TO TAKE THIS IGNORANT BANDIT INTO OUR CAREFUL CUSTODY.

BEHAVE UNTIL WE LEAVE. AM. I. CLEAR?

WHAT ARE YOU DOING HERE!?

EVEN THOUGH I WAS BORN A ROYAL...

...I WAS NEVER ALLOWED TO DO ANYTHING.

NOT EVEN TO KNOW THINGS OR LEARN THINGS.

I FINALLY GOT OUT OF THE PALACE, AND I STILL CAN'T GET 'EM TO LET ME HANDLE ANYTHING!!

I NEVER KNEW THE REAL WORLD WAS LIKE THIS.
MY PEOPLE ARE SUFFERING, AND I...!!
I...
WHAT WAS I BORN A PRINCE FOR ANYWAY!?

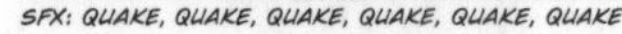
SFX: QUAKE, QUAKE, QUAKE, QUAKE, QUAKE, QUAKE

...IS THE ONE GIFTIN' THIS BOOZE TO MY ROYAL FOLKS?

THIS SAME MAN WAS ALSO LEFT IN CHARGE OF THE VILLAGE'S PERIODIC REPORTS.

IT WOULD SEEM THIS MAN REDIRECTED THE WATER TO ONLY HIS FIELDS...
...IN ORDER TO BUILD A GREAT STOCK OF WINE AGAIN.
THE PRIEST'S FARM SHOULD BE INSIDE THE "TEMPLE."
IT IS TIME FOR JUDGMENT.

LET'S TEACH 'IM A LESSON.
LET'S HURRY UP AND TEACH THAT PRIEST!
USELESS ANUBIS SERVANTS...

LISTEN!! THIS PRIEST DUDE IS A DOWNRIGHT EVIL VILLAIN!!
SHALL I STRIKE YOU FOR REAL?
THAT GUY...!!
MY PARENTS WERE WORKIN' ON THE FARM... BUT...

ONE DAY, NEITHER OF 'EM CAME HOME...

A MESSENGER OF THE PRIEST CAME AN' TOLD ME...THERE WAS AN ACCIDENT WHILE THEY WORKED.

AN ACCIDENT...!!

THEY WOULDN'T SAY ANYTHIN' ELSE...!

THEN TELL ME—WHY DO YOU THINK THE ROYAL FAMILY HAS NOT INTERVENED IN THIS INCIDENT!?

BECAUSE THIS VILLAGE HAS BEEN UNDER THE RULE OF THE PRIEST-HOOD!!!

!!?

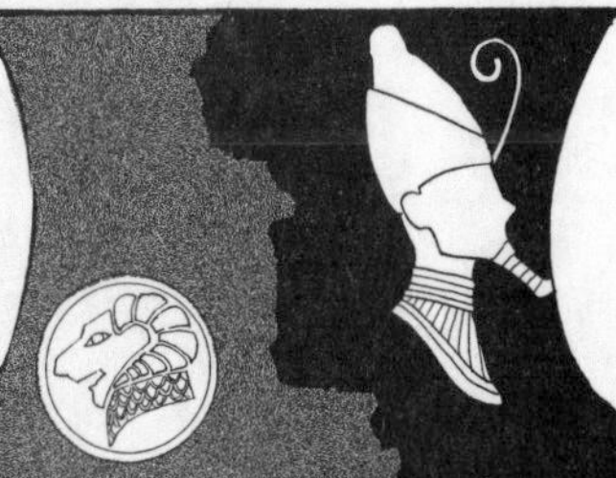
WE PRIESTS HAVE SERVED THIS KING-DOM WITH CONSTANT DEVOTION.
YET YOUR FATHER SMEARED OUR GOOD NAME. EVER SINCE HE CALLED US TRAITORS, THE KINGDOM HAS BEEN SPLIT IN TWO.
THIS VILLAGE WAS ABANDONED BY THE PHARAOH AT THAT TIME. IT IS ONLY ONE OF THE VILLAGES THAT WAS GOVERNED BY US IN THE PRIESTHOOD!!

...!!
DID ANYONE KNOW OF YOU?
THE PEOPLE OF THIS VILLAGE LEARN LITTLE OF THE ROYAL FAMILY.

THE REVERSE HOLDS TRUE AS WELL.
IN FACT, THE MAJORITY OF THE VILLAGERS SUPPORT THE PRIESTHOOD.
RELYING ON THE ROYAL FAMILY LIKELY NEVER EVEN CROSSED THEIR MINDS.

EVEN IF THEY HAD DONE SO, WOULD THE ROYAL FAMILY HAVE STEPPED IN?
...LEAVING A PRIEST'S FAULT IN THIS DISGRACEFUL INCIDENT OUT OF IT, ALLOW ME TO TELL YOU THIS— THERE IS NO TRUST HERE.

THE FEUD BETWEEN THE ROYAL FAMILY AND THE PRIESTHOOD IS THROWING THE KINGDOM INTO CHAOS!
THE PEOPLE DO NOT KNOW ON WHOM TO DEPEND. THIS IS BECAUSE THERE IS NO CLEAR RULER.

MY IGNORANT PRINCE...

OUTSIDE, THIS IS THE REAL WORLD.

...WHAT CAN I DO...?

IF YOU WISH TO DO SOMETHING, THEN GO HOME IMMEDIATELY, AND MAKE THIS REQUEST.

"IF THIS INJUSTICE TRULY HURTS YOUR HEART, THEN WHEN YOUR TIME COMES, I WANT YOU TO GIVE THE THRONE OVER TO THE PRIESTHOOD." ASK IT OF YOUR ELDER BROTHER.

SURELY YOU CAN HANDLE THAT MUCH?

... FINE.

IF YOU CAN'T COUNT ON MY OLD MAN OR MY BIG BRO!!!
THEN I'LL BECOME PHARAOH, AND BRING THE KINGDOM TOGETHER!!!
JAB
AND I'LL GET STARTED AFTER I BLOW THIS BAD GUY SKY-HIGH!!!
ZOOM
WH—!?
STOP!!! DJOSER!!!
...YOU FOOL...
...YOU CAN NEVER...
...BECOME PHARAOH ...NOT YOU...

GUAH!
WHACK
H...HOW DARE A LOWLY BRUTE...
...RAISE HIS HAND AGAINST A PRIEST!!
SHUT UP!! YOU'RE THE BAD GUY HERE!!
SEND THE WATER TO THE VILLAGE, RIGHT NOW!!!
TAK
AH!
YOUR HOLI-NESS... LORD IMHO-TEP!!!
PLEASE, SEND THIS CRIMINAL TO HELL!!!

EFFECTIVE IMMEDIATELY, YOUR POSITION AS PRIEST IS REVOKED.

I WILL CAST YOU TO THE OTHER SIDE OF HELL'S GATE.

TCH!

DASH

...WHY YOU ...!!

DON'T GET IN MY WAY!!

SHRRK

THUD

SNORT

THUD

THUD

WHAT IS THAT THING !!?
!!
SURELY YOU KNOW WHERE YOU ARE!?
THIS IS THE TEMPLE OF THE GOD KHNUM, WHO CONTROLS THE FLOW OF THE NILE!!
SNORT
GREAT PRIEST OR NO, YOU CANNOT TOUCH THIS HOLY RAM, THE AVATAR OF KHNUM!! IF YOU KILL IT, YOU WILL BE THE CRIMINAL!!
SLAP
BOOOAAAAAAAAA
RUN HIM DOWN !!!
THUD
THUD
THUD

...A LIVING GOD— A ROYAL— IS PERMITTED TO DO SO.

THUD

SCRAPE

!?

.....WHAT!!?
YOU'RE GONNA TAKE RESPONSIBILITY FOR THIS, RIGHT, IM...!?
BULGE
FLING
SMASH
KRAK
GYAAAH!!!
RAAAM!!!
YOU OKAY!!? SORRY 'BOUT THAT!!
WORRY NOT. I WILL HEAL IT.

OKAY!!
TIME FOR YOU TO FIX THE RIVER!!!
......GAH!

...HA-HA-HA-HA!! TRY AND UNDO IT, IF THAT'S WHAT YOU WANT!
?

I MAY HAVE STARTED OUT AS A FARMER, BUT I'M A REAL PRIEST TOO!!
I STEADILY HONED MY MAGIC! OVER THE COURSE OF MORE THAN TEN YEARS, I PUT MULTIPLE LAYERS OF SPELLS ON THE VILLAGE AND TEMPLE'S WATERWAYS!!
AND IT SEEMS I HAD CONSID-ERABLE TALENT FOR IT!!
OH, YOU'LL FIND IT TO BE STRONG WORKMAN-SHIP!!!

BY MY CALCULATIONS, THE PROCESS IS SO COMPLICATED THAT IT WOULD TAKE ANY OTHER MAN FIFTY YEARS TO UNRAVEL!!
HAHAHAHAHAHA!

I AM NOT A MONSTER!! I GIVE THE VILLAGERS EMPLOYMENT ON MY FARM, AND I EVEN PAY THEM A FAIR WAGE!!

ONE LITTLE VILLAGE NO LONGER GETTING WATER WON'T CHANGE THE KINGDOM'S PRODUCTIVITY!!

THOSE WHO LIVE IN A WORTHLESS VILLAGE ARE ALSO WORTHLESS!

WHO CARES ABOUT THAT STUPID VILLAGE!?

CAN YOU DO IT IN FIVE *MINUTES*?

FIVE *SECONDS*.

I'M ALREADY DONE.

BOOM

ZSHHH
WATER!!!

THERE ARE CROPS FLOATING DOWN-STREAM TOO!!!
IT IS A MIRA-CLE!

KHNUM HADN'T ABAN-DONED US!!

LORD IMHO-TEP!!

IT IS THE POWER OF LORD IMHO-TEP!!!

WELL, THEN.
ZZZ.
MY SERVANTS WILL BE HERE SHORTLY. THEY WILL TAKE YOU TO OUR HEAD-QUARTERS. DO NOT RESIST.
TAK
TAK
TAK
WE ARE RETURNING TO THE VILLAGE.
DJOSER.
"DJOSER"...!?
DO NOT TELL ME YOU'RE *THAT* "PRINCE DJOSER"...!?
THE ONE AND ONLY!!!
FINALLY, SOMEBODY WHO KNOWS ME!!!
YOU'RE LOOKIN' AT THE MAN WHO'S GONNA BE THE NEXT PHARAOH!!!
HUH!?
!?
AH HA HA HA HA HA HA HA HA!

PHA-RAOH!!?
OH, YOU PITIFUL THING...!!
YOUR FATE IS ALREADY SET IN STONE...!!!
THE VERY MAN BEHIND YOU...
HE WILL...

KRAK

...IM THREW A PUNCH? WHOA...

I'M NOT MAD ABOUT HIM LAUGHIN' AT ME, Y'KNOW?

DO NOT MISUNDERSTAND.

...IF YOU NEED ANYTHING, TELL THE ANUBIS.
ZSHHH

THANK YOU, LORD IMHOTEP!
YOU'RE OUR SAVIOR!!
YOU SHOULD BECOME THE LORD OF THIS LAND!! PLEASE!!
STAY WELL!!
HEY, BANDIT BRAT!! DON'T YOU GO MAKING TROUBLE FOR LORD IMHOTEP, GOT IT!?

THANK YOUUU!
LORD IMHO-TEEEP!!
GAAAH! I TOLD YOU, I'M NOT A BANDIT!!
DAMMIT! I HELPED TOO!
HERE! A GIFT!!
!!

WHISPER
THANKS, PRINCE!!

NO PROB!!
TAKE CARE, KID!!

THANK YOUUU! LORD IMHOTEEEP!!

GOOD THING THAT KID'S PARENTS...
...WERE ONLY BEING HELD PRISONER, SO THEY GOT HOME SAFE, RIGHT?
......

...I WAS WRONG TO SAY SUCH AWFUL THINGS TO YOU.
HUH?
CREAK

THIS AFTERNOON. I TREATED YOU LIKE A FOOL...
WHY ARE YOU APOLO-GIZING?

I DIDN'T KNOW ANYTHING, BUT YOU WERE NICE ENOUGH TO LET ME IN ON THE TRUTH, RIGHT?
HONESTLY, I SHOULD BE THANKIN' YOU!!!

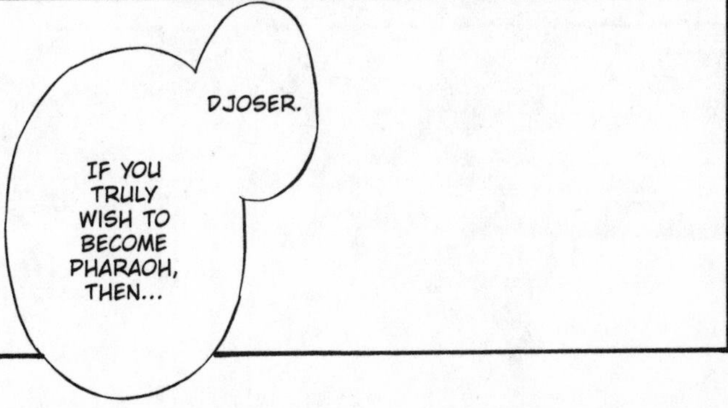
DJOSER.
IF YOU TRULY WISH TO BECOME PHARAOH, THEN...

...YOU WILL HAVE TO CREATE A KINGDOM...

...IN WHICH THERE ARE NO WICKED PEOPLE. ONE IN WHICH I DO NOT HAVE TO CAST ANYONE INTO HELL.

...
...I SEE...
HONESTLY, THAT SOUNDS WAY TOO FRIKKIN' HARD...

BAM
...BUT I HAVE THIS FEELING I CAN PULL IT OFF, IF I'VE GOT YOU!!!

SO COME ON!!
LIFT

HUH!!!?

KEEP TEACHIN' ME MORE STUFF!!
IT'S YOU AN' ME!!
IM!!!

THE HERO WHO SAVES HIM...

...IS THE GREAT MOON PRIEST WHO STANDS BY HIS SIDE.

IM 11 END

AFTER ♀ WORD

HELLO!! I'M MAKOTO MORISHITA!! THANK YOU SO VERY MUCH FOR READING UNTIL THE VERY END!!!

THANKS TO YOUR SUPPORT, I WAS ABLE TO DRAW AN EPIC STORY SPANNING ELEVEN WHOLE VOLUMES—MORE THAN ENOUGH!!!

"WORSHIPPING THE READERS" POSE

FOR THE FINAL AFTERWORD, I'D LIKE TO WRAP THINGS UP WITH SOME DETAILS ABOUT THE TWISTS AND TURNS OF THE CREATION OF *IM*, AND BEHIND-THE-SCENES STORIES.

2010

MY FIRST MANGA SUBMISSION, "RAVEN CAGE": SQUARE ENIX MANGA PRIZE RUNNER-UP & MY DEBUT

SUDDEN

A STORY ABOUT A BOY WITH MULTIPLE PERSONALITIES AND A DARK ANGEL GIRL

IT WAS GOING SO WELL—TOO WELL—THAT AT FIRST I THOUGHT THERE'D BEEN SOME KIND OF MISTAKE AND THAT I SHOULDN'T BE GETTING EXCITED.

I'M SHIMOMURA. I LOOK FORWARD TO WORKING WITH YOU!

OH, THANK Y—ERR...UM... JUST TO DOUBLE-CHECK, AM I REALLY...?

YES, YOU'RE THE RUNNER-UP.

ULP...

A COLLEGE FRESHMAN AT THE TIME

I FINALLY BELIEVED IT WAS REAL WHEN I WAS INVITED TO THE AWARD CEREMONY LATER.

↑ NAUSEA FROM NERVES

HOWEVER...JUST BECAUSE I MANAGED TO DEBUT, IT DIDN'T MEAN EVERYTHING WOULD FALL INTO PLACE... AND AS I WAS A HUGE WORRIER, THE PRESSURE OF JOB-HUNTING FEVER AROUND ME GRADUALLY WORE ME DOWN.

FROM: YOUR EDITOR

"You haven't been sending in storyboards lately. I'm concerned. You've said you're considering finding a full-time job. I'll be straight with you—being a manga artist is no walk in the park. Now is the time for you to decide whether to give up on being a manga artist."

TAK TAK TAK

THAT WAS WHEN!!!

REPLY:

"I'll quit job-hunting."

ANCIENT EGYPT EXHIBIT

A HARSH BUT ALSO KIND COMMENT. THE MOMENT I RESOLVED TO LIVE UP TO THOSE EXPECTATIONS, I TOOK MY JOB-HUNTING AND TOSSED IT OUUUT!!!

BEING AWAY FROM MANGA FOR A LITTLE WHILE HAD ACTUALLY CLEARED MY MIND.

AND THAT WAS WHEN I SAW IT.

↑※ THIS IS THE EXTREME DIGEST VERSION. IT WASN'T SUCH A LIGHT BACK-AND-FORTH.

2013
チン DING
I FINISHED IM (THE PILOT CHAPTER).
SO ROUGH!!
HEROINE OF THE PILOT CHAPTER, EMI
AFTER THAT, I DREW ONE MORE ONE-SHOT STORY, AND IN OCTOBER OF 2014, WHILE I WAS WORKING AS AN ASSISTANT TO YOU OMURA-SENSEI (ARTIST OF ROSE GUNS DAYS SEASON 3)——...
OH YEAH. MORISHITA-SAN, HOW ARE YOUR STORYBOARDS COMING ALONG?
OMURA-SENSEI
...I'VE DRAWN THREE CHAPTERS' WORTH, BUT...
...LAST TIME IT WAS ALL NIXED.
I HAVEN'T GOTTEN A REPLY ON THIS PITCH YET, SO IT MIGHT GET ALL REJECTED AGAIN.
RIGHT AFTER I GOT HOME
HOW FAR HAVE YOU GOTTEN ON THE MANUSCRIPT FOR CHAPTER 1??
(EDITOR)
?
...WHAT IS THIS PERSON SAYING ...??
MY SERIALIZATION HAD BEEN GREENLIT WITHOUT ME KNOWING.
(FOR REAL.)
THE FACTS: THE SERIALIZATION GOT GREENLIT BECAUSE THE READER SURVEY RESULTS FOR THE ONE-SHOT WERE GOOD (ACCORDING TO THE EDITOR).
IS THIS HOW DRAWING A SERIES STARTS FOR EVERYONE...??
JUST MOVED IN, SO NO LIGHT
AFTER I RUSHED THROUGH DRAWING CHAPTER 1 ON MY OWN:
ME: "UM! I DON'T HAVE A ROOM FOR ASSISTANTS!"
EDITOR: "THEN RENT AN APARTMENT FOR ABOUT TWO WEEKS, AND FIND SOME ASSISTANTS!"
ME: "WHAT DO I DO FOR CH. 2 IN THE MEANTIME...?"
EDITOR: "DRAW IT, OF COURSE!"
I DON'T REMEMBER THE TASTE OF THE RICE I ATE OR ANYTHING.
THE SERIES STARTS NEXT WEEK...
NO HEAT, SO WEARING TWO COATS.
A ROUND TABLE AND FLASHLIGHT I BROUGHT FROM MY PARENTS' HOUSE
THE FIRST THING I BOUGHT WAS JUST CURTAINS.
AND IN JANUARY 2015, IM BEGAN SERIALIZATION!!!
IT WAS A CHAOTIC START, BUT DURING THE SERIALIZATION, WE DIDN'T MISS A MONTH OR TURN A CHAPTER IN LATE EVEN ONCE!!!
I HAVE MAJOR RESPECT FOR ARAKAWA-SENSEI!! AFTER SHE GAVE ME ADVICE TO NOT RELY ON ENERGY DRINKS AND GET MORE SLEEP, I HAVEN'T HAD EVEN ONE ENERGY DRINK!!!
MSSP.
IT'S ALL THANKS TO MY ASSISTANTS.
MORNING OF JUNE 18, 2018: NORTH OSAKA EARTHQUAKE
ALTHOUGH THE FINAL CHAPTER—THAT WAS THE ONE CHAPTER I THOUGHT WE WOULDN'T GET DONE IN TIME.
CHUKKA CHUKKA CHUKKA CHUKKA
*HELICOPTER SOUNDS
A MAGNITUDE 6 EARTHQUAKE IN OSAKA...!? YIKES... THERE'S HELICOPTERS HERE...
OH, BUT MY ASSISTANTS ARE ALL OKAY... THANK GOD...
THE TRAINS AREN'T RUNNING!!!
ガチャリ KCHAK
GOOD MORNIIING...
ASSISTANT WHO BIKES TO WORK
MSSP.
Y-YOU CAME HERE IN THIS STATE OF EMERGENCY!!?
I THOUGHT I'D FEEL SAFER HERE THAN AT HOME ALONE!!!
IT WAS A FINAL CHAPTER WE OVERCAME AS A GROUP.
AFTER THIS, WE WENT OUT TO BUY WATER AND FOOD TOGETHER. BUT THERE WAS ALREADY NONE LEFT. (IT'S IMPORTANT TO KEEP A REGULAR STOCK!!)

FINAL THOUGHTS

HE GOT TO LIVE TO ADULTHOOD.

NEW WORLD ROUGHS

HARUGO, AGE 25

GRADUATE STUDENT MAJORING IN FOLKLORE STUDIES AND MYTHOLOGY

BOTH HIS PARENTS ARE ALIVE AND WELL.

HIMEKO, AGE 18
ASPIRING PASTRY CHEF

WADJITYUUTO, AGE 18
OIL MAGNATE (LOL)

RUSTLE
サラァ…

ALL THREE SIBLINGS ARE LIVING HAPPILY TOGETHER.

KOBUSHI, AGE 20
ILLUSTRATOR
OFTEN WORKS AS A TEAM WITH HINOME

FOR YOUR BOOK COVER? LEAVE IT TO ME!

SO THEY ARE BOYS LIKE THIS...

HINOME, AGE 20
PICTURE BOOK AUTHOR

SLOPPY...

INABA, AGE 25
FORMER TRACK & FIELD ATHLETE
↓
NURSERY SCHOOL TEACHER (DATING A GIRLFRIEND WITH MARRIAGE IN MIND)

SHAMS
BAKER
AGE 22

HEY, DON'T SLEEP ON THE JOB...

MAKOTO MORISHITA

もりしたまーと

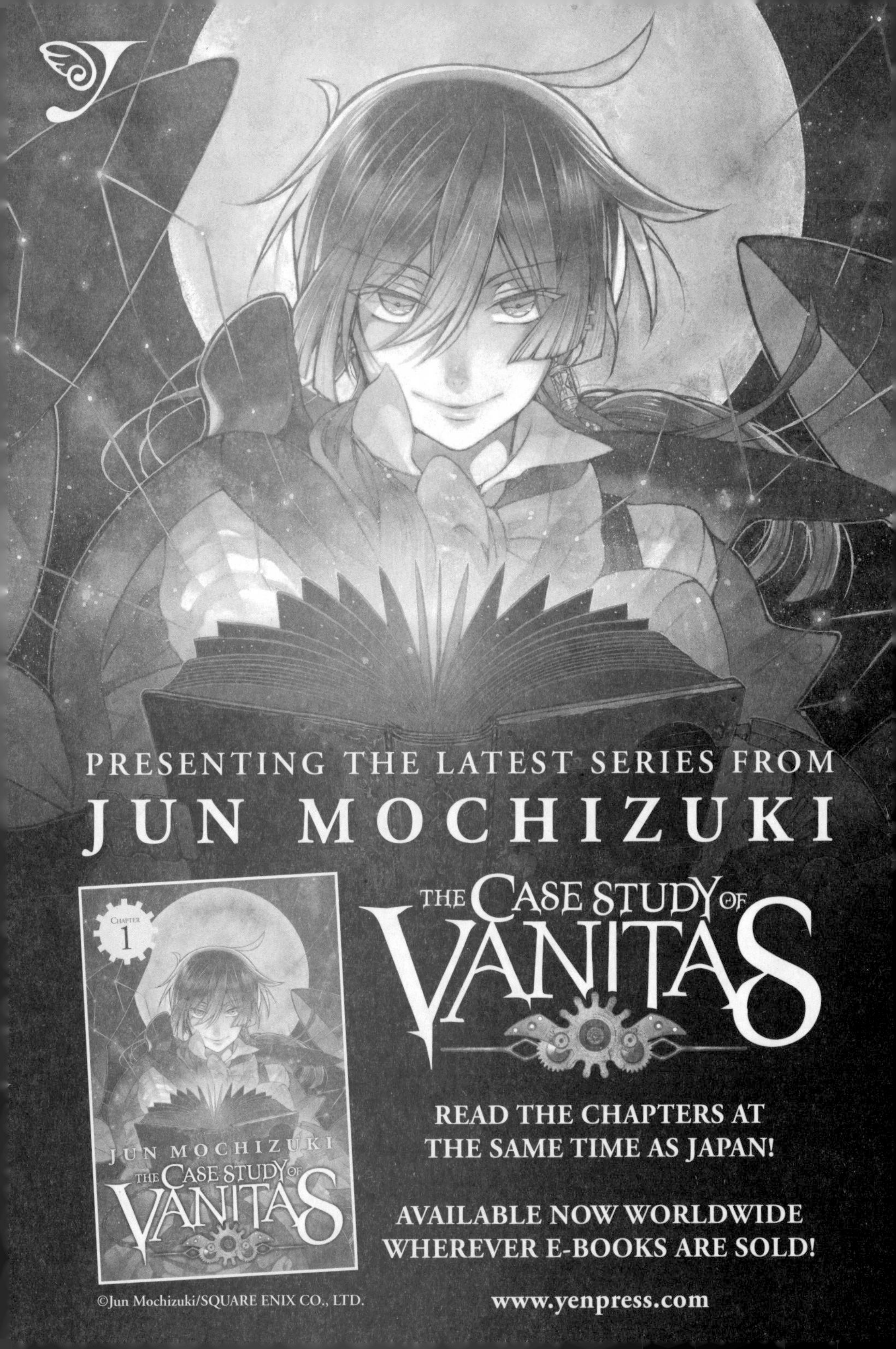

HE
BREAKS
HEARTS,
NOT
DEADLINES!
MONTHLY GIRLS'
NOZAKI-KUN
IN STORES NOW!
Yen Press
YenPress.com

HORIMIYA ©HERO • OOZ ©Daisuke Hagiwara / SQUARE ENIX
Yen Press
HORIMIYA
VOLUMES 1-15
HERO × DAISUKE HAGIWARA
A sweet "aww"-inspiring tale of school life begins when two similarly dissimilar teenagers discover that there are multiple sides to every story...and person!!!
Visit YENPRESS.COM
TO CHECK OUT THIS TITLE AND MORE!
IN STORES NOW!

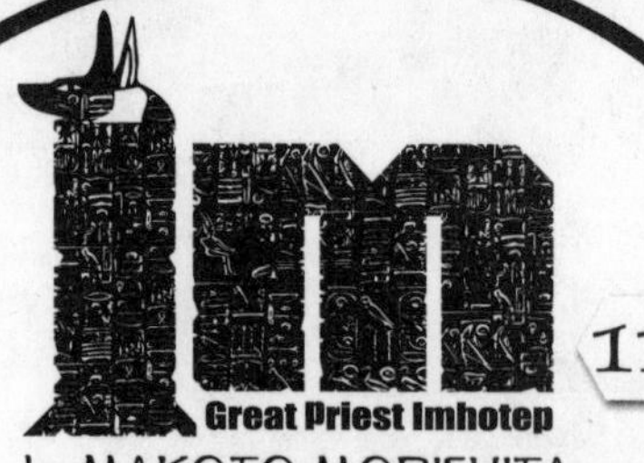

by MAKOTO MORISHITA

Translation: Amanda Haley
Lettering: Rochelle Gancio

Yen Press
150 West 30th Street, 19th Floor
New York, NY 10001

Visit us at yenpress.com facebook.com/yenpress
twitter.com/yenpress yenpress.tumblr.com
instagram.com/yenpress

First Yen Press Print Edition: September 2021
Originally published as an ebook in February 2019 by Yen Press.

Yen Press is an imprint of Yen Press, LLC.
The Yen Press name and logo are trademarks of Yen Press, LLC.

The publisher is not responsible for websites (or their content) that are not owned by the publisher.

Library of Congress Control Number: 2019953326

ISBN: 978-1-9753-1152-0 (paperback)

10 9 8 7 6 5 4 3 2 1

WOR

Printed in the United States of America